FEEDEM FIGHTERS

GW00707356

A Comedy

By Dorian Mode

Published in the UK and Ireland by PLAYSTAGE
www.playsforadults.com

On behalf of ORiGiN™ Theatrical
Part of the ORiGiN™ Music Group –
An Australian Independent Music Company
www.origintheatrical.com.au

LANGUAGE NOTE

Licensees are welcome to make small alterations to the language that is used is this play so as to make it suitable for a younger cast and/or a local audience.

MUSIC NOTE

Licensees are responsible for obtaining formal written permission from copyright owners to use copyrighted music in the performance of this play and are strongly cautioned to do so. If no such permission is obtained by the licensee, then the licensee may only use origin music that the licensee owns and controls.

www.playsforadults.com

Designed by Kate Lowe, www.creative-mix.co.uk

FEEDEM FIGHTERS

CAST *(In order of appearance)*

DARYL
: 40+, overweight likeable soft-drink salesman, trying to divorce his two-timing wife. Believes junk-food is proof God wants us to be happy.

SHONA
: 40+, determined, cynical, former hard-core university radical looking for meaning now communism is dead. Believes the only thing men and sperm have in common is a one in-a-million chance of becoming a human being.

KEVIN
: 40+, idealist, naive, dubious sexuality, always looking for the good in people but being perpetually disappointed. Earned his 15 mins of fame as the biggest winner on The Biggest Loser. Once sent money over the Internet to a Nigerian Princess called Brian to unlock secret funds.

GARY
: early 30s, brawny, muscled, ex-SAS, skin-head haircut, more hair than brains. Obsessed with discipline, king-sized chip on his shoulder, enjoys bullying people, pines for the regimen of army life.

BERNICE
: *(VIDEO ONLY)* 40+, botox, fake-nailed, bottle-blonde, conniving, vindictive cougar with a fake tan and too much jewellery.

DOUG*
: early 30s, ex-army, good natured.

PARIS*
: early 40s, outrageously camp dance teacher, fit, lithe, dry, sarcastic.

CHAN*
: *(VOICE ONLY)* highly-strung local restaurateur on the point of a nervous breakdown

2 females (1 on video), 6 males (but 3 of the parts could be doubled and 1 of those parts is voice only)

The action takes place in a spartan, soundproof one-roomed apartment in a city in the UK. The time is the present

FEEDEM FIGHTERS

ACT 1

SCENE 1

SOUNDPROOF ROOM – DAY OR NIGHT

*The theatre is dark. The audience hears whispered pleas from the stage.
"Help me!" "Help me!" "Call the police!" We hear mysterious Arabic music.
As the audience settles, a spotlight is raised on DARYL, who is wearing a
loud lumberjack shirt, jeans, cheap trainers, bound with rope, lying on the
floor with a hood over his head – hands bound behind his back, feet chained.
The stage is bare, save for an exercise bike, a TV/DVD player, and a full
length mirror and height chart. We watch our hostage writhe on the floor for
several mysterious minutes, pleading in desperate whispers for the audience
to call the police. Suddenly a light snaps on in the room and a door opens on
the set. DARYL becomes suddenly quiet. KEVIN, GARY and SHONA –
dressed like urban freedom fighters – enter wearing balaclavas, 'hoodies' and
camo trousers.*

GARY speaks aggressively in Arabic to the hostage.

SHONA   *(interrupting, annoyed)* That's an evil thing to do, Gary.
             Stop it now! And turn that creepy music off!

             (GARY walks over to the CD player and kills the music).

GARY   God! Where's your sense of humour? I'm only mucking about!

SHONA   Take the hood off him, Kevin. And I hope you didn't gag
             him, Gary. The last one was an asthmatic. Lucky you didn't
             kill him.

             *(KEVIN removes the hood. DARYL looks up from the floor,
             frightened and confused.)*

DARYL	Kevin?? Gary??? So...you guys aren't Arab terrorists?
GARY	*(sarcastically)* Yeah, a South London soft drinks rep is an Al Qaeda priority. You and the US President have been on our top ten hit-list for years.
DARYL	Really??
GARY	What do you think, arsehole?
DARYL	I did sign a petition about stopping a Mosque going up in Fulham but I was pissed and eating a hot dog outside the football stadium. *(Thinks.)* So if it's not terrorism, what's it all about? *(Thinks some more.)* Haaang on! Are you people tied up with Coke?
SHONA	*(irritably)* Do we look like drug dealers?
DARYL	No no...I mean, Coca-Cola. I've been making inroads into their line of sparkling colas and lemon teas for some years now, particularly in Streatham. Thought something like this might happen after I stuck my sign over theirs outside Jimmy's Greek restaurant in Clapham High Street. Jimmy warned me. "Don't take on the multinationals. You'll never win."
GARY	*(to SHONA)* Jesus. Can you believe this, dude? We've nabbed some morons in our time but this guy takes the biscuit.
KEVIN	Shall we tell him?
	(They nod. KEVIN pulls out a tuning pipe and blows a note and nods to the team. SHONA exits and returns with a birthday cake.)

SHONA,
GARY,
KEVIN

Happy Birthday to you, Happy Birthday to you, Happy Birthday dear Daryl...Happy Birthday to You!

(GARY places a paper hat on DARYL on the floor. KEVIN pulls the string on a party streamer. It pops and shoots over his fettered body on the ground. GARY pops the cork on a bottle of champagne and the three pour themselves a drink, turning their backs on DARYL. SHONA cuts slices of cake. They chat amiably amongst themselves about the ease of the operation. DARYL looks on from the floor, incredulously.)

DARYL

Um, I'm sorry to interrupt your little party over there but what the hell is happening to me?

KEVIN

(drinking) This is your birthday present, Daryl. Cheers!

DARYL

My what?

(SHONA whips out some paperwork from a large black bag.)

SHONA

(reading) Did you or did you not tell your wife on April the third of this year, while watching the report on us on Sky News, that you wished Feedem Fighters would snatch you off the street so you could fit into your old tux for Brian's wedding in December?

DARYL

(sotto voce) Oh crap...

GARY

(reading) And did you or did you not also add that you would – and I quote – "sell your soul to lose five stone" – that's 31.751 kilos.

DARYL

(sotto voce) Oh God...

KEVIN

And didn't your doctor also warn you that if you didn't lose at least forty pounds by the end of the year, you would be dead by 50?

DARYL   My doctor is twenty stone. I'll outlive *him*!

GARY   Blimey! That's 127.005 kilos! We must send him a brochure.

SHONA   *(shows him a contract)* Tell me. Is that your signature?

DARYL   Yes but...I signed that when I was pissed. I remember now! Bernice said it was for some Weight Watchers course...

SHONA   Welcome to your birthday present, Daryl.

DARYL   But I asked for a watch!

KEVIN   *(excitedly)* This is better than any watch, Daryl! *(KEVIN walks over to a large rip-off-the day style wall calendar to reveal today's date.)* This is the first day of the rest of your life. Welcome to the new Daryl!

DARYL   But I'm not that unhappy with the old Daryl.

KEVIN   You won't be saying that in three months when you look in a mirror and smile at your new body.

DARYL   Three months! Three bloody months!! You have to be kidding!!

SHONA   Your wife must love you very much.

DARYL   Oh, yeah, she loves me, alright. She'll be terribly depressed with me out of her life for three months. Probably at the hairdressers right now sipping champagne in mourning.

             (SHONA pushes DARYL to the floor.)

SHONA   Sexist.

DARYL   Fact, sweetheart. My wife cuts her hair more than Sinead O'Connor.

SHONA   Don't call me "sweetheart". It's patronising.

DARYL   Oh, hey, I'm sorry to make you uncomfortable. What was I thinking? Me bound up on the floor. You must feel humiliated.

SHONA   This is all for you, Daryl. You'll understand in the end.

DARYL   Well, thanks very much for all this. You know...for the kidnap and bundling me in the boot of your car and everything. I mean, it's really sweet but I'm cancelling your contract, forthwith.

GARY   *(standing over him)* It doesn't quite work that way, Fatso. Your wife also has a contract with us. You walk, she sues. Simple as that.

DARYL   Who do you think pays the bills?

SHONA   Sexist.

DARYL   Fact. My wife hasn't worked since we got married.

SHONA   And I suppose cleaning and ironing and cooking, isn't work?

DARYL   No, it's work. But she has a cleaner who cleans, an ironing lady who irons and we mostly eat out - hence the extra kilos.

SHONA   Sounds like a modern woman.

DARYL   Futuristic.

            (KEVIN sets up a video camera. GARY and SHONA grab DARYL and face him toward the camera.)

DARYL   What's he doing? What...what are you doing?? What's the camera for?

GARY   He's videoing you for the reveal.

DARYL   The reveal?? What am I some kind of renovation show?

SHONA   *(pointing to camera)* Okay. Action. Now, what do you have

to say to your wife who's shelled out for this top shelf
Feedem Fighters executive package for your 40th birthday?

DARYL   *(to camera)* Just this. *(leans in to camera)* I'll get you for
this, Bernice! I'll really get you for this, you bitch!

GARY   They all say that on the first day. Shock mostly.

KEVIN   *(videoing)* You'll feel bad about saying that in three months,
Daryl. You really will. You'll ask us to take it back. They
all do.

DARYL   What are you talking about??

SHONA   And.........Cut!

*(KEVIN stops filming and nods to GARY. GARY feeds a
DVD into a machine. Suddenly footage of a bejewelled
fake-tanned bottle-blonde, sipping champagne at the
hairdressers, appears on screen.)*

BERNICE   *(from TV)* Well happy birthday, Daryl! I know you wanted a
watch, babe, but I thought 'what can I buy you that tells
you how I really feel about you?' for the big four-o. So I
looked through your E-mail and found a message to Di
that told me everything.

DARYL   She knows.

SHONA   Knows what?

DARYL   It's code. Never mind.

BERNICE   *(from TV)* So I chose this gift for you. Now don't fret! I've
told work you are taking compassionate leave to visit a sick
relative in Australia...

DARYL   No, no, no, no, noooo! I've got customers relying on me!

BERNICE   *(from TV)* Meanwhile...I'm taking our son Christopher on a long holiday to the Italian Riviera. He sends his love, bless him.

DARYL   You rotten bitch!

SHONA   That's sweet.

DARYL   Sweet?? Christopher is her Pilates instructor! We don't have any kids.

BERNICE   *(from TV)* ...so I'll bring you back a souvenir, darling. Probably a watch. I won't buy you any clothes because they tell me I won't recognise you after three months of rice cakes and water and gruelling fitness regimes. Now, I've left a suitcase full of your clothes with the team. Love ya, babe!

             (They switch-off the DVD. The three smile serenely at DARYL, still bound and on the floor.)

DARYL   Can't you see what this is all about?

SHONA   Um...let me think...Bernice wanting to save your life?

DARYL   Save my life? You mean bleed my bank account dry and piss off with her toy boy, while I'm chained up here, more like it.

SHONA   That's an exaggeration, Daryl. We've heard them all before. Kevin! The Fattie Fib List, if you please.

             (Kevin pulls out a sheet of paper from a black bag.)

KEVIN   *(reading)* I'm due to give evidence in court on Thursday. I'm a diabetic and need insulin urgently. I'm an asthmatic. *(Turns to SHONA)* That turned out to be true. I should scrub that from the Fattie Fib List.

             (DARYL bellies his way to the door. GARY drags him back.)

GARY   *(to DARYL)* Get back here piggy...

KEVIN   *(continuing to read)* I've got to perform vital surgery on

	Monday. I'm leading a golf tournament and if I don't make the green by three I'll lose the championship for the club.
SHONA	*(to KEVIN)* That was Malcolm wasn't it?
KEVIN	(to SHONA) Yeah, I really liked Malcolm until he licked my soup from the floor that day. He lost my respect after that.
SHONA	*(to KEVIN)* I've seen 'em hungry before, but he was crazed with hunger.
KEVIN	*(continuing to read)* I have jury duty. I'm a professional wrestler and have a championship bout on Wednesday night-
SHONA	That was Carl. He was pretty tough.
KEVIN	Yeah, remember he got you in a headlock for that doughnut?
	(KEVIN puts SHONA in a mock headlock.)
SHONA	Yeah, I had to wrench his testicles. *(Pretends to wrench KEVIN's testicles.)* His BO was the worst.
GARY	I had to zap him with my cattle prod.
SHONA	I was in control! Had his boys in my hands the entire time.
DARYL	*(struggling to his feet)* You use a cattle prod!??
GARY	Not anymore, sadly. This was a little beauty, too. Plugged straight into your household power socket and delivered just enough volts to make you scream but...
	(SHONA blows a whistle. They stand to attention.)
SHONA	Professionalism, Gary! *(to DARYL)* Gary's ex Special Forces. He was in the SAS.
GARY	Afghanistan. Covert ops mostly.
DARYL	*(to himself)* These people are psychos.
KEVIN	*(continuing to read)* I'm claustrophobic. My husband's

divorcing me and bought this package because he hates me. *(to DARYL)* Sound familiar, Daryl? I'm a chain smoker.

GARY   *(holds up a pack of cigarettes)* Me too!

KEVIN   *(continuing)* I suffer with sleep apnoea and need my machine.

SHONA   Until he lost weight!

KEVIN   *(continuing)* I'm pregnant...

DARYL   You kidnapped a pregnant woman?? You're kidding, right?

SHONA   She wasn't pregnant. She was just fat.

DARYL   Sexist.

SHONA   You can have two rice crackers for dinner or just one, Daryl. Keep the wisecracks coming. *(to KEVIN)* Any others?

KEVIN   Just one. I have a faecal discharge problem *(they all laugh)* but he really did have a faecal discharge problem. That was literally a shitty gig.

             (They all laugh. SHONA blasts her whistle.)

SHONA   Professionalism, Kevin? You don't tell the client everything. *(to DARYL)* So in other words, *(grabs DARYL's chin)* we've heard every excuse ever invented by a cunning, fat, lazy mind.

DARYL   But here's the thing. I'm not really that fat.

             (They regroup in a corner and chat amongst themselves.)

KEVIN   *(to SHONA softly)* I was thinking that.

GARY   *(quietly)* Me too, just quietly. I mean he's overweight but he'd have to be the skinniest one so far.

SHONA   *(to DARYL)* Okay. How much do you weigh, exactly?

DARYL	*(panicky, thinking)* Um...eh...15 stone.
GARY	That's 95.254 kilos.
DARYL	Good with numbers are we, Rambo?
SHONA	You're a liar, Daryl.
DARYL	It's true!
SHONA	*(to GARY)* Gary. The scales.
	(GARY snaps to attention and whips out a set of scales from the black bag.)
GARY	Let's find out, shall we? Get on them scales, Lard Boy.
DARYL	How can I? I'm bound up like Hannibal Lecter. At least undo my feet for Chrisesakes.
KEVIN	Last time we did that Shona was kicked in the teeth by a nasty client.
SHONA	*(rubs her jaw)* True.
GARY	*(to KEVIN)* Yeah, old Elsie was quite agile, wasn't she?
KEVIN	Gary had to take her down.
SHONA	Not before I socked her in the jaw with a left hook. Should have seen those dentures fly. That stopped the old bitch lashing out in her sensible shoes.
DARYL	*(sotto voce)* Holy crap.
	(GARY and KEVIN drag DARYL to the scales.)
SHONA	Sounds tough but she was going to die, Daryl, she was so overweight. As a thank you present in the end, she knitted me a camouflaged cardigan. *(SHONA squeezes his crotch. DARYL winces.)* You lash out with your feet Daryl and I'll have your balls for earrings. That's a promise. Got it?

DARYL   (*soprano*) I get the message! (*GARY unties his legs. DARYL gingerly steps on the scales. He unwisely decides to be light hearted*). Normally, I have to buy a woman a glass of wine first. You're rather attractive when you're mean.

(*At this comment, SHONA wrenches his testicles, then 'sets the boys free'. SHONA reads the scales over his shoulder. But DARYL has his foot on the display. She grabs his 'boys' again till he moves his foot away. DARYL screams.*)

SHONA   15 stone, eh? That says 120 kilos Daryl.

GARY   That's 18.896 stone, Fatso.

SHONA   How do you expect us to believe your wife is hiring us as some kind of marital revenge when you can't even be honest about your weight?

DARYL   The scales are wrong!

(*Suddenly KEVIN hits a large button on the wall. A siren goes off. The stage flashes with red. SHONA pulls out a large cardboard sign from the black bag. It reads: THE SCALES ARE WRONG*)

DARYL   Very clever. But I'm telling you they are bloody wrong.

SHONA   Gary. The sugar.

(*GARY produces a packet of sugar from the big bag.*)

SHONA   How much does the packet say, Daryl?

DARYL   (*sighs*) One kilo.

GARY   (*grabbing him by the balls*) Sorry, pal. We can't hear you.

DARYL   (*louder*) ONE KILO! Rambo doesn't have your soft hands, Shona.

(*They place the packet of sugar on the scales. It reads 'one kilo'.)*

GARY	*(sneeringly)* What does it say, Fatso?
DARRYL	Okay. So I lied about my weight. But I'm not lying about my wife setting me up so she could run off with her Pilates instructor.
KEVIN	You're missing the point, Daryl. This is about the new you. The new trim, healthy Daryl. Shona, can we play him the testimonials, now?
	(SHONA nods. The team play him a DVD with photos of the 'before clients'. The footage melds into a pastiche of cheesy music and teary thankyous from newly trim clients.)
DARYL	Is that supposed to make me feel better or something?
KEVIN	It's to show you the big picture. To give you a goal. Something to work towards. An end game.
DARYL	Well, I don't know if it's escaped your attention but did you see a little theme with those people in that video?
KEVIN/SHONA	What theme?
DARYL	All of those people are morbidly obese. Like I said, I'm not that fat. If I cut back on the beer and junk food...
KEVIN	*(quietly)* He's got a point, Shona. He'd never make the final casting of Biggest Loser.
GARY	*(reading a chart)* Ok. BMI index time. How tall are you, Maggot? *(GARY lifts him by the hair to his feet.)*
KEVIN	Sorry, Daryl. It's a commando training thing.
DARYL	*(panicky thinking)* Six two.
GARY	That's 188.98 centimetres. *(GARY shakes his head in disgust.)*
SHONA	Get out the height chart, Kev. *(KEVIN drags him over to a*

height chart on the wall. SHONA speaks in a tired voice)
Stand against the wall, Daryl.

DARYL Okay okay. I'm five ten. Happy. But I'm still not obese.

GARY Right! Drop em and give me fifty.

DARYL Fifty what?

GARY Fifty push ups.

DARYL Piss off.

GARY Kev, go fetch my cattle prod.

DARYL My wrists are bound, for Chrisakes. What do I push up with? My tongue?

GARY *(reading a booklet)* According to the body mass index you are morbidly obese.

DARYL The BMI? That thing's a con and everyone in the world knows it. Probably invented by the Swiss. They're flawed, the Swiss. Look at the war. Even their cheese is full of holes.

SHONA The BMI index is a medical standard.

DARYL According to the BMI, Kate Moss is obese.

KEVIN We always go off the BMI. Sorry Daryl. Company policy.

DARYL And who officially sanctioned that? The Terrorist Arm of Weight Watchers? Do you know how many laws you're breaking here?

  (KEVIN slaps the wall-button. Siren goes off and the stage flashes with red. SHONA flips over a sign on the wall which reads: DO YOU KNOW HOW MANY LAWS YOU'RE BREAKING?)

DARYL Hang on. Hang on. I remember now... Weren't you guys in court – according to Sky News - for taking a woman hostage and nearly killing her. Hang on!! And she was pregnant! That's right! She was bloody pregnant!! You people are psychos.

SHONA   Thrown out of court.

DARYL   Why?

(SHONA shows him the 'after picture')

DARYL   She looks kinda hot. I don't get it. Why nab her?

SHONA   This is what she looked like before she was gifted the Deluxe Safari Package by her step-father. *(SHONA shows him the 'before' picture.)*

DARYL   Geeze! What a Blimpasorous! Okay, I admit that's some transformation.

KEVIN   *(to the others)* That's the Safari Package for you. It delivers.

DARYL   So what does the hostage…

SHONA   …'Client'

DARYL   …'hostage' get for his money if he coughs for the Safari package?

GARY   We kidnap you. Bundle you into the boot of a car…

KEVIN   …Landrover…

GARY   I've told you before - a Landrover doesn't have a boot!

KEVIN   But it has more of a 'safari aesthetic' than a Toyota Camry.

GARY   Listen Kevin, I've told you…

(SHONA blows her whistle)

SHONA   We then take you up in a light plane. Put a parachute on you - attached to Gary -throw you both out of a plane and leave you on a remote desert island for three months.

KEVIN   Gary takes a rubber dingy from the island to the mainland
                 and radios the client each night to tell them where the
                 rations are buried.

GARY   *(sinisterly)* If you are a good boy or girl for Uncle Gary, that is.

SHONA   Otherwise they'd eat it all at once. No willpower.

                 *(The three punch their chest, salute Black Panther style,
                 shouting 'WILL POWER')*

DARYL   *(dryly)* So why didn't I get the Safari Package? I can only
                 imagine Bernice's delight as I fall from the sky, blindfolded,
                 screaming, while strapped to this raving lunatic.

GARY   Mosquitoes. Outter season.

DARYL   *(sotto voce)* Wonder she didn't insist.

KEVIN   Anyway, in court, Liz broke down - that's the client - and
                 admitted she became pregnant *after* losing the weight.

SHONA, GARY *(to KEVIN)* Hmmm. *(They nod knowingly to each other as
                 if there is more to the story.)*

KEVIN   You see, that was one of her goals. To have a baby. Doctor
                 said that to fall pregnant she had to lose eighty kilos.

DARY   Eighty?

SHONA   Eighty.

GARY   Yeah, and hubby wasn't going to bone her looking like the
                 great White Whale of Wimbledon. Should have seen her on
                 that island. Like a stranded walrus. "I need foooood, Gary!"

SHONA   *(hitting GARY in back of head)* That's sexist, Gary! And not
                 very professional in front of the client. I don't like that kind
                 of language used about women. It's degrading.

GARY   I'd say the same thing if Liz was a bloke.

SHONA	But you never do, Gary. That's the point.
GARY	I'll bloody well say what I want, Shona! I was in the Special Forces. I used to give the orders. Not take them, remember?
SHONA	Well, that was then. This is now. So shut up, Gary.
GARY	Don't tell me to shut up. And besides it's 'Commando' remember? We all agreed. I was to be called 'Commando'.
KEVIN	But it's too derivative of The Biggest Loser Gary. I thought we talked about that. We need originality. New ideas.
GARY	We're not creating a work of art, Kevin. It's a business.
DARYL	Whoa whoa whoa! I hate to interrupt the charming Abu Ghraib canteen banter, but you haven't answered my question...
ALL	What?
DARYL	These other 'clients'...they're morbidly obese.
	(They look sheepishly at each other.)
DARYL	I'll admit. I'm slightly overweight. Big boned. A little cuddly in budgie smugglers.
	(They detonate with laughter.)
SHONA	*(laughing - patting his bum)* I'm trying to imagine you in budgie smugglers! Geeze!
DARYL	*(winks)* I thought there was a twinkle in your eye.
GARY	Right! You heard that, Kevin. That's sexist. You're a witness. She wouldn't say that if it was a woman in a bikini.
SHONA	Oh, shut up, Gary.
	(They argue amongst themselves.)
DARYL	I heard that too, Gary. I think you've reached an impasse.

Clearly you'll have to release me and dissolve the company.

KEVIN   Guys! Guys!! GUYS!!! See what he's doing? *(to DARYL)* Ooo! You're good, Daryl. I'll give you that. Normally the client tries to turn us against each other in the third or fourth week. I can see we're going to have to watch you. *(to others)* I know! Let's go out for a celebration curry and have a glass of wine and celebrate a successful lift. Gary, tie our client to the chair.

DARYL   Oh, great. You go out for a curry while I'm left handcuffed to the table with a bloody rice cracker.

SHONA   Three.

DARYL   Generous.

(They motion to leave.)

GARY   And don't think of yelling, Daryl. *(Crouches behind DARYL and speaks to him over his shoulder.)* I designed this room meself. In here, they can't hear yer scream. Acoustic batting. Lead lined giprock - known in the trade as SoundCheck…

DARYL   And what trade is that? Psychos, Painters and Torturers?

GARY   …acoustic seals imported from Germany…

DARYL   Apt.

GARY   …and that skylight is triple-glazed. You couldn't smash it with a brick. In fact, one client broke his fist trying.

KEVIN   He's very proud of his work.

DARYL   Pol Pot speaks highly of him.

SHONA   We'll be back in two hours.

DARYL   Can you at least leave that TV on? Football's on at nine.

SHONA   You have to earn privileges.

DARYL   Earn TV?

KEVIN   The more weight you lose, the more TV you're allowed.

DARYL   Funny. In real life, it's the other way around.

               (The three leave)

DARYL   *(shouting after them)* Can you bring me back a Butter
               Chicken and some Naan bread!

               (BLACKOUT)

DARYL   *(in the darkness)* ARE YOU GUYS SERIOUS? YOU'RE
               JUST GOING TO LEAVE ME TIED UP FOR TWO
               HOURS? *(pause)* I'M NOT OBESE. JUST FAT AND
               HAPPY !!! *(pause)* I'LL SUE YOU FOR THIS! *(Longer
               pause)* PRICKS!!!

               *(In the darkness we hear a medley of cheesy jingles from
               fast-food commercials or food-related song.)*

END OF SCENE 1

ACT 1
SCENE 2 COOKING SCHOOL

Lights are raised. The stage now has a portable chopping table. KEVIN, sporting an apron and small chef's hat, is gaily chopping vegetables on a bread board. DARYL, apron and chef's hat, is chopping perfunctorily, pissed-off and bored. The giant calendar on a wall of the set reveals it's three weeks later.

KEVIN   *(chopping enthusiastically)* Now, the secret to losing weight is eating more, would you believe? Eating more!!

DARYL   *(chopping half-heartedly)* You're kidding, right?

KEVIN   No, I'm not. If you eat healthy food, but more of it, rather than snacking in between meals, you'll lose stacks of weight.

DARYL   Really?

KEVIN   Sure. It's knowing *what* to eat. *What* to drink. Avoiding the bad stuff. I mean, you sell soft drinks right?

DARYL   Yeah. So?

KEVIN   Well, I bet you drink the product all day because it's free.

DARYL   One of the perks.

KEVIN   False economy! Why not simply drink bottled water instead?

DARYL   Pay for water?? Ever spelt 'Evian' backwards?

KEVIN   What about diet drinks?

DARYL   I hate that saccharin aftertaste.

KEVIN   You'd get used to it. Now chop this coriander for me. We are going to use the stalks as well as the leaf in this dish.

DARYL	So if I stop drinking soft drinks, I'll lose weight. Got it. Can I leave now? *(motions to leave)*
KEVIN	*(laughing)* Keep chopping.
DARYL	*(holds the knife at KEVIN)* What's to stop me putting this knife to your throat, ripping the swipe card off your neck, and making a dash for it?
KEVIN	One word.
DARYL	Gary?
KEVIN	Gary.
DARYL	But he's not here.
KEVIN	*(laughs)* Never leaves his post. On these jobs he lives in a caravan out front. The corridor is alarmed and wired with CCTV. He has the entire place booby-trapped. Before you're down the stairs and out the door, he's introducing you to a world of pain. It's ugly. You don't want to go there, trust me. You see, I *inspire* my clients to lose weight. Gary *tortures* his clients to lose weight. Remember the cattle-prod??
DARYL	He doesn't have a cattle-prod, does he??
KEVIN	*(giggling)* Nah, we made him get rid of it.
DARYL	Where did you dig this psycho up from?
KEVIN	We found him after he auditioned for Biggest Loser as a trainer but he wasn't quite what they were looking for.
DARYL	How surprising.
KEVIN	Now, have you cooked stir-fry before?
DARYL	Sure.
KEVIN	What do you do after preparing the vegetables and lean meats?

DARYL   Fill the wok with oil.

               (KEVIN slaps the siren and holds up a sign which reads:
               POUR OIL INTO THE WOK/PAN)

DARY   The siren is a little over the top, don't you think?

KEVIN   (tapping his forehead) Psychology. It's to remind you not to
               make excuses about your weight when you leave. Fatties are
               the sum of their excuses.

DARYL   So how do I stir-fry without the 'fry'?

KEVIN   Simply spray the wok lightly with vegetable oil.

               (DARYL sprays the wok.)

DARYL   Won't it simply burn all the food?

KEVIN   Not if you use a non-stick wok.

               (DARYL studies KEVIN's face.)

DARYL   You know...I've been thinking...You look familiar. Have I
               seen you on television?

KEVIN   (smiling to himself) I don't think so.

DARYL   Sure?

KEVIN   You've mistaken me for someone else.

DARYL   I know! It must have been Sky News.

KEVIN   We were all wearing balaclavas, if you remember.

DARYL   Yeah, you're right...

               (There is a twinkle in KEVIN's eye.)

KEVIN   So you spray the wok lightly with oil...

DARYL   Ever audition for Britain's Got Talent?

KEVIN   (smiling to himself) Then you crush the garlic. But don't let
               it burn.

DARYL	UK Border Force? Ever smuggle small goods in your good smalls?
KEVIN	Now grate the ginger. Ginger is medicinal. Great for upset tummies. Not that you'll have too many of those if you stick to my dieting program...
DARYL	Ever wear sequins on Strictly Come Dancing?
KEVIN	(smiling) Avoid big chunks of ginger because they can be bitter.
DARYL	Hang on! I've bloody got it! I've got it!! If I was to imagine you say 200 pounds heavier and wearing an oversized shirt with the words Biggest Loser on it, would I be close?

(KEVIN grins but keeps cooking.)

| DARYL | That's it! That's bloody it!! Well, what can I say? I'm truly in the company of flabby greatness! You are, in fact, 'Kevin the Florist' - otherwise known as 'Mr Miracle'! No one has ever lost as much as you on Biggest Loser! |

(KEVIN blushes and shrugs.)

DARYL	Wow, I hardly recognise you! I used to say to Bernice, 'I bet that bloke puts it all back on as soon as he leaves the studio.' Well, how about that! So you kept it all off, eh?
KEVIN	Every pound. Now can you chop that capsicum? A lot of vitamin C in capsicum. More than oranges would you believe?
DARYL	Well, it's a credit to you, mate. You look great. I mean, by the last episode you looked like a giant scrotum with all that excess skin. So what motivated you to keep it all off?
KEVIN	A suit.
DARYL	A suit?

KEVIN   Long story.

DARYL   I'm not going anywhere. Especially anticipating the first
             decent meal I've had since you bundled me into the boot of
             your car, kidnapped and humiliated me. So what happened?

             (KEVIN sighs and regards DARYL with a tired look.)

DARYL   Come on, you know you want to tell me.

KEVIN   I wouldn't know where to start.

DARYL   Try the beginning.

KEVIN   *(sighs)* Ok. Well, I can see you're not going to let it rest.
             (Pushes the chopping table aside and moves centre stage.)
             I've always had trouble with my weight. Ever since
             childhood. I attended a very exclusive school in London
             where image was everything. But I was the chubby kid boys
             would argue over after picking two football sides as to who
             would be stuck with me. All part of my self-esteem program.

DARYL   Kids can be cruel.

KEVIN   You don't know the half of it.

DARYL   Go on.

KEVIN   School was hell. So I was dreading my year 12 school
             formal. That is until one of the prettiest girls in the school
             asked me to take her to the dance. Couldn't believe my luck!

KEVIN   All the cool guys congratulated me. When I got home that
             day and told Mother I had a date lined up, well, she was
             absolutely beside herself with excitement.

             (DARYL sits down to listen, eating a carrot stick.) We went
             shopping for a suit. Hard buying a suit being my size back
             then. It's as if big people didn't exist under the age of 21. In

the end, Mother made me a suit based on a design we found in a British fashion magazine. It hid the pounds well.

DARYL   She made you a suit?

KEVIN   Mother's clever like that. I must say, it was a hit. She even had Stephan of Stephan's Glamour Photography take my photo.

DARYL   I've seen him on the shopping channel peddling his wares. You pay three grand to look like the star of a soft porn movie.

KEVIN   That's him! Very talented. Anyway, on the big day, I don't know who was more nervous. Mother or me. I borrowed Uncle Harry's E-type Jag so I could pick up my date in style. God, I could hardly fit in the seat. Ever sat in one?

DARYL   Everyone was really thin in the sixties. All that post war austerity.

KEVIN   True. Well...I drove to Camilla's house - my date - but she wasn't there. Her mother met me at the door. She was clearly disappointed in her choice of chaperone. I could see the disdain on her face as she looked me up and down. Her mother said she'd stayed over a girlfriend's house the night before and was planning to meet her date at the dance. When I arrived at the dance, my classmates dragged me through the crowd of dancing teenagers to her. That's when I saw her.

DARYL   Stunning?

KEVIN   Not quite.

DARYL   What then?

KEVIN   She was wearing a fat suit.

DARYL   A fat suit? Wow, that's low.

KEVIN   Really?? Everybody thought it was hysterical. She took it off to dance with her real date. Josh. Captain of the rugby team.

DARYL   That's an awful story, Kev.

KEVIN   Tried to take my own life that night. Even failed at that. Never told Mother. She still thinks the night was a triumph.

DARYL   Sad story.

KEVIN   That's the life of a fat boy, Daryl. Were you fat at school?

DARYL   Nah. Only put it on when I gave up fags.

KEVIN   Happens.

DARYL   So what about your date? Did she ever apologise? Later in life?

KEVIN   She wrote to congratulate me on winning Loser. Shedding all the pounds somehow made me human again. One of the gang.

DARYL   What was in the letter?

KEVIN   *(shrugs)* It was a well-crafted letter, dodging responsibility, without an apology, full of spin, you know...justifying her actions.

DARYL   What a bitch! What does she do for a living these days?

KEVIN   Speech writer for Tony Blair.

DARYL   Figures.

KEVIN   When I started to put the weight back on after Loser–as you inevitably do, simply by re-hydrating, and because you don't have the pressure-cooker situation–like you're in now –I found Mother's suit stuffed in the back of the wardrobe. It was all the motivation I needed. From that day forward, if I felt hungry, I thought of the suit.

DARYL   But aren't you playing into their hands?

KEVIN   What do you mean?

DARYL   The weight police. I mean, why should we have to lose
            weight to be accepted into society?

KEVIN   I want to be accepted into society. We all do.

DARYL   By who? A bunch of spoilt public school pricks? And why
            do we have to conform to what the media tells us is the right
            or wrong way to look? In Elizabethan times, poor people
            would blacken their teeth because only the rich could afford
            sugar. What does it all mean in the end? Image? Is it really
            who we are? Deep down? Do we all have to look like
            clones?

KEVIN   But it's a health issue, too, Daryl.

DARYL   What's healthy about losing 20 pounds in a week on Biggest
            Loser? Any doctor will tell you it's dangerous. One of those
            contestants will drop dead from a heart-attack one day.

KEVIN   They surely will do if they don't stop over-eating. Being
            overweight shortens your life, Daryl. It's a fact.

DARYL   According to who? According to those people who tell you
            that you will die because you're too fat as they puff on a
            filtered cigarette like Rambo down there. The same people
            who take packets of laxatives to fit into a new dress. Gimme
            a break! I'm as healthy as any of them. Healthier!

KEVIN   So you are saying being fat is a political statement?

DARYL   All I'm saying is that those shows like Biggest Loser are
            simply manifestations of the same bullying you experienced
            at school. You don't have to humiliate people because they
            look like crap in swimming trunks. There will come a day
            when all of us will look like crap in budgie smugglers. See

what I mean?

KEVIN   I see your point.

DARYL   *(motions for the door)* Good. Then let me out of here, now.

               (Dramatic pause as KEVIN thinks.)

KEVIN   Ahh, I see what you are doing, Daryl! *(returns to cooking)*
               You're good. I'll give you that. *(taps forehead)* Psychology! I
               can see we're going to have to watch you. You get people
               talking, talking, talking, get them to open up about
               themselves and then you twist it to suit your own purposes.
               To make good your escape. You're cunning. I'll give you
               that.

DARYL   God! Who are you people? Al-Qaeda? I'm making a point
               about body image. I'm not questioning the validity of Islam.
               All I'm saying is that I'm happy with the way I look now. I
               don't need to be thin to be happy. I like me. The fat happy
               me.

KEVIN   *(stops cooking)* Mother always said: "You can never be too
               thin or too rich".

DARYL   Tell that to Karen Carpenter.

KEVIN   Fair point. *(With a loud sigh, KEVIN returns to the cooking.
               DARYL picks up the wok.)* You must have some money to
               afford this dieting retreat.

DARYL   *(incredulous)* Dieting retreat?? Is that what you bloody call
               it??? What do you call Guantanamo Bay? A Cuban holiday
               with free clothes?? Besides, I'm not paying for this. My
               bloody wife is. With my money. MY MONEY! If I had the
               cash I'd be off to Bali eating nasi goreng cooked in woks
               filled with duck fat. She's only done this to have a dirty

holiday with her toy boy!

KEVIN   *(chopping)* I'd like to believe you, Daryl. I really would. But I'm afraid I can't. You see, I've heard it all before. You'll thank us in the end. They all do. Imagine your wife...

DARYL   ...ex-wife!

KEVIN   ...your 'ex-wife' seeing you trim and terrific!

DARYL   Yeah, but I'm not some hot twenty something Pilates instructor, either. Can you make me into one of those?

KEVIN   You'll have to settle for trim and terrific.

(DARYL paces.)

DARYL   Bloody Bernice! She's always been one of those women who prey on young men. What's the word for them? Jaguars!

KEVIN   Cougars.

DARYL   Cougars? Oh, that's very American. We need a British version of that, don't we? What could it be...? What's that scruffy dog that all the toffs have, that goes hunting?

KEVIN   Lurcher?

DARYL   Perfect! She's one of those lurchers.

KEVIN   *(laughing)* I like it.

(DARYL picks up the can to spray the wok again but it's faulty. It won't spray.)

DARYL *(looking at can)* You know I think this is playing up.

KEVIN   Let's have a look.

(KEVIN walks over as DARYL sprays him in the eyes with the can.)

KEVIN   *(covering his face)* OH GOD! WHY DID YOU DO THAT?

DARYL   I'm sorry, Kevin. You seem like a nice bloke and everything with your fat suit story but I have to get out of here. Now where's your swipe card??

             (DARYL snatches the card from a chain around KEVIN's neck and swipes the door. He quickly exits the stage. We hear the SIREN. Stage flashes red. We hear an FX ELECTROCUTION NOISE. Stage lights dim and flicker.)

DARYL   *(Offstage)* AHHH! FOR THE LOVE OF CHRIST!

GARY   *(Offstage)* GET BACK UP THEM STAIRS, LARD ARSE!

DARYL   *(Offstage)* This'll be used in evidence against you in a court of law! I hope you realise that, you creepy Psycho! It'll all come out at the trial. The cattle-prod. Everything! ARGHH! JESUS!!!

             (DARYL enters the stage slightly smoking. His hair is standing on end, like a porcupine. KEVIN wipes his eyes with a tea towel.)

KEVIN   *(wiping eyes)* That was a foolish thing to do, Daryl.

DARYL   Thought you were bluffing about Rambo!

KEVIN   *(wiping eyes)* No. I mean spraying something in someone's eye like that.

DARYL   Gettoff! It was only vegetable oil. Won't kill you.

KEVIN   You're really going to cop it from Gary, now, I'm afraid. This means we can't trust you. You'll lose privileges.

DARYL   *(sotto voce)* Shit.

             (A steel box rings on the table. KEVIN fingers a combination lock to open it and answers a mobile phone.)

KEVIN   *(to mobile–little boy's voice)* Shona? No, I'm fine. I'm fine.

Yes, Daryl's fine.

DARYL   Fine? FINE?? I'm smoking like a fucking barbequed chicken! Tell her what he did to me. Tell her what he did.

KEVIN   *(quietly into mobile)* Gary still has the cattle prod. *(pause)* I know, he told me he took it back, too.

(DARYL stalks KEVIN around the chopping table threatening him with a wok.)

DARYL   Who to? Hannibal Lecter??

KEVIN   *(to mobile)* No, I'm okay. Just a little vegetable oil in my eye. Yes, yes. At least he didn't stab me like Malcolm did that night.

DARYL   Stab you? And upset Shona? I'm used to my testicles being where they are.

(DARYL still stalks KEVIN).

KEVIN   *(to mobile)* Okay. Okay. I'll tell him.

DARYL   Does she know I can sue you all over this? BIG TIME!! Does she know? Tell her! Tell her that.

KEVIN   *(to mobile)* Yes, I'll tell him, Shona.

DARYL   Does she know this is totally illegal? An invasion of my civil rights. Remind her of that. Tell her. Tell her now!

KEVIN   *(to mobile)* Yes. Yes. I'll tell him. I'll tell him.

(KEVIN slams the table into DARYL - winding him. DARYL buckles in pain. KEVIN ends the call and locks the mobile phone into the safety box and places the box under the sink.)

KEVIN   *(to DARYL, yelling)* Shona says she is extremely disappointed in you for spraying me in the eye with the vegetable oil. She says she's warned you about desperate tactics. And the consequences.

DARYL   *(sarcastically)* Oh, I'm terribly sorry to upset her. I feel just awful.

KEVIN   She says if you try anything like that again, she will not be held responsible for Gary and his 'trust punishments'.

DARYL   'Trust punishments?'

KEVIN   She's on her way over. Now you're in for it. Gary's *easy*.

DARYL   It was just harmless vegetable oil made from 'rape' otherwise sold under the marketing-friendly name 'vegetable'.

KEVIN   Really? Vegetable oil is really made from rape?

DARYL   Made from rape seed. But 'Sussex – Rape County of Great Britain' just didn't quite work on the signs, apparently.

KEVIN   Well, it was a silly thing to do, nonetheless.

        (We hear a buzz on the intercom. KEVIN buzzes the person in. SHONA enters with a bag of groceries, flustered.)

SHONA   Thanks, Kev. Go home and bathe your eyes. I'll cover you.

        (SHONA grabs the vegetable oil and sprays DARYL in the eyes. DARYL shrieks.)

SHONA   *(to DARYL, yelling)* This could plunge him into another depression, you know. He has a lot of issues surrounding trust!

DARYL   *(incredulously, wiping eyes)* Oh, I'm so sorry, Shona. I wouldn't want Kevin to feel betrayed or depressed after holding me hostage for a month.

KEVIN	(to SHONA, furious) See what I mean? This is what I'm working with. (calmer) Call me at home later. Ciao.
SHONA	Ciao.
KEVIN	Ciao.
	(KEVIN leaves. We hear a scream off stage as lights flash. We hear an FX electrocution noise as the stage lights dim and flicker.)
KEVIN	(offstage) GARY , YOU LUNATIC! WHAT DO YOU THINK YOU ARE DOING?
GARY	(offstage) Sorry Kev. Thought it was Fatso making another run for it.
KEVIN	(offstage) SHONA, WILL YOU MAKE HIM SEND BACK THAT FREAKING CATTLE PROD!
	(SHONA throws all of KEVIN's cooking in the trash.)
DARYL	Hey, hey! What are you doing? That's my dinner!
SHONA	You are kidding? After what you just pulled? He trusted you. It's rice cakes for you, Daryl Lucas. If you're lucky.
DARYL	Let me get this straight. I reach my goal weight in a few weeks, I'm outta here. Next time we meet is in court, right?
SHONA	You reach your goal weight in two weeks, I'll eat my hat.
DARYL	Right now, I'd share it with you because I'm STAAARVING!
	(SHONA wipes down the cooking bench.)
DARYL	(sotto voce) I'll make the weight, don't worry. Then I'll have my day in court. That's my goal.
	(SHONA pulls out a book from her handbag and curls up on the seat to read it. DARYL puts a rice cracker on a plate

and eats it with a knife and fork.)

DARYL   *(eating)* Whacha reading?

SHONA   *(reading)* Gabriel García Marquez. Something that wouldn't interest you. Literature. Postmodernism.

DARYL   *(eating)* One Hundred Years of Solitude? Or Love in the Time of Cholera? If it's Cholera, the butler did it.

SHONA   *(shocked)* What do you know of postmodernist writers?

DARYL   *(eating)* I have a degree in English Lit. Hence me selling soft drinks in South West London.

(SHONA puts down her book.)

SHONA   You? English Lit? I don't get it.

DARYL   It's very simple. In my first week at Reading University I was sitting on the student bog. Above the toilet roll was written these salient words: Arts Degree. Please take one.

SHONA   Never would I have picked you as a book person.

DARYL   Even wrote one.

SHONA   Yeah right...

DARYL   *(still eating)* Well, nearly twenty years ago.

SHONA   Published?

DARYL   Sure.

SHONA   How many did it sell?

DARYL   Not many.

SHONA   How many's not many?

DARYL   Nothing. Thirty thousand copies.

SHONA   Bull. Shit.

DARYL	True.
SHONA	I know you're big on the psychology as a quick route out of here Daryl but this is pretty desperate. I can easily check this out.
DARYL	It's out of print now so you can't buy it, unfortunately.
SHONA	Convenient.
DARYL	But you'll find it in most libraries.
SHONA	Okay. What's it called? I'll call your bluff and find it.
DARYL	A League Imbeciles. Should have dedicated it to you three.
SHONA	I'll try and find it at my local library. What's it about?
DARYL	Read it and find out.
SHONA	(chuckling) You're a king sized bullshit artist, Daryl. You think feigning an interest in books and trying to pretend you were an author is going to get me to weaken my guard or something and let you slip away. You really are pathetic.
DARYL	You can find it in most libraries.
SHONA	(chuckles to herself) Yeah, right. You crack me up sometimes. You really do.
DARYL	You have a nice smile for a kidnapper. Have I ever told you that? In a Joseph Goebbels kind of way.
SHONA	(reading, smiling) Eat your crackers, Daryl. I'm immune to your charms.
DARYL	Dumb and Dumber might buy that but there's a spark between us. I make you laugh and it scares the shit out of you.
	(SHONA, reading, looks worried. DARYL sidles up beside

her and breaks his cracker in two.)

DARYL   Cracker?

BLACKOUT

(In the darkness we hear Olivia Newton John's 'Physical' as the set is modified by stage hands)

END OF ACT ONE.

FEEDEM FIGHTERS
ACT 2
SCENE 1 EXTREME SAS TRAINING

Lights are raised. Part of the stage is transformed into a home gymnasium. DARYL is pedalling on a stationary bike with GARY scribbling on paper at the table, periodically yelling at him.

GARY	Come on, Lard Boy. Faster. Faster, you worthless maggot!
DARYL	What are you doing over there, Gary? The Census?
GARY	Something your lazy fat mind wouldn't be interested in.
DARYL	Try me.
GARY	A Japanese number puzzle. Sudoku *(GARY pronounces it "sad-oku")*. Ever heard of it?
DARYL	I know it by its English translation.
GARY	*(looks up, keenly)* Really? What's that?
DARYL	"Sad-bloke-ooo."
GARY	Pedal!
DARYL	You love numbers, don't you Gary?
GARY	Less talk and more pedalling, Fatso.
DARYL	I'm pedalling as fast as I can.
GARY	*(screaming over him)* If the Taliban was chasing you with an AK 47 you'd be pedalling for your life. I can assure you of that, my fat friend.

(DARYL stops and turns to him.)

DARYL	But that's just the thing, Gary. They're not. I'm simply locked in a soundproof room with rice crackers and an ex Special Forces psycho screaming at me while doing Sudoku.
GARY	*(menacingly)* Shut up and use your imagination.
	(DARYL pedals.)
DARYL	Right now I'm imagining sitting by my favourite river, with my fishing rod, a book and a couple of cold beers, after a cheery afternoon spent visiting you all in jail.
GARY	Tell me. How much beer do you drink a night, Daryl?
DARYL	Nothing really. Dunno. A six pack.
GARY	A six pack?? That's your fat problem right there! Know how many carbs there are in beer?
DARYL	Never really worried about it.
GARY	What about diets? Tried many?
DARYL	I don't diet. I keep telling you. I like being fat. However, Bernice had me on that new Hollywood seafood diet last month.
GARY	*(taking notes)* How does it work?
DARYL	Well, you eat salmon the first night. Oysters the following night. Wednesday is tuna sashimi. Mussels and sardines on the Thursday, followed by fresh king prawns and smoked eel on the Friday. Weekends you can either have dressed crab, smoked trout, lobster or lightly grilled marinated squid. You do that, with subtle variations, for a month.
GARY	Lost much?
DARYL	No. But my wallet lost over ten kilos.
GARY	You're in the soft drink business. You must drink a lot of

soft drinks. Did you know there are 8 teaspoons of sugar in every can of Cola?

DARYL   Not my company's Cola. There's only five and a half.

GARY   So your company is introducing healthier soft drinks?

DARYL   Nah, they're just cheap bastards.

GARY   Your pedal rate is fading.

DARYL   So is my will to live.

(We hear a buzz on the intercom. GARY answers it.)

GARY   *(to intercom)* Who is it?

DOUG   *(offstage.)* Buzzards fly west in June.

GARY   But often fly east in May.

DOUG   *(offstage)* Squawk.

GARY   Squawk.

(We hear the clumping of feet on the stairs. GARY's ex-army chum, DOUG, walks in eating an oversized frosted doughnut.)

DOUG   *(to GARY)* So who's the latest torture victim?

DARYL   Hi, I'm Daryl.

(DARYL hops off the bike and steps over to shake DOUG's hand but GARY seizes DARYL in a commando hold.)

DARYL   Otherwise known as Lard Boy, Lard Arse, Fatso, Fat Man, Maggot and sometimes, if Gary is hungover, "You-lard arsed-fatboy-maggot" - but only on formal occasions.

GARY   Keep pedalling, Maggot. You've got another twenty minutes.

DOUG	*(to GARY)* How much has Daryl got to lose? He doesn't look that fat.
GARY	Only thirty pounds to go. But he's only lost 5 this week. Can't understand it. This special op should have been a breeze. Must be a genetic thing with this one.
DOUG	Maybe he's just a born fatty. Some people are like that.
DARYL	I am in the room. Fat person with feelings pedalling!
GARY	Don't worry. We know. We can smell yer.
DARYL	*(pedalling)* Charming. *(DARYL looks up at the skylight with a curious look on his face.)*
DARYL	Woah! *(They follow his gaze and all look up, DOUG still eating his frosted doughnut.)*
GARY	What is it?
DARYL	Nothing. *(DARYL looks up again and pulls a face. He slows his pedalling.)*
GARY	What is it?
DARYL	It's just...
GARY	*(snaps to action)* Is someone on the roof?
DARYL	Well, I thought I saw... Nah, must be my imagination. *(The three look up at the skylight.)*
GARY	I'll take a look and make a surveillance report for Shona. *(GARY puts on a massive collection of SAS equipment, including a balaclava)*
DARYL	What's all that get up for?
GARY	Might need to take someone out.

DARYL	What? On a date?? What do you mean 'take someone out'?? You're not in Afghanistan, Gary. You're in fucking Whitechapel.
GARY	*(quickly turning to DARYL)* How the hell do you know that?
DARYL	Because this fool is wearing a tag saying Whitechapel Electronics.

(DOUG looks down at his staff tag and tucks it into his shirt. GARY scowls at him, shaking his head. DOUG shrugs in mute apology.)

GARY	*(to DOUG)* Keep a close eye on him, soldier, while I do a surveillance of the area. Watch him. He's shifty, this one.
DOUG	Okay. But I have to be back at work in twenty minutes. Kylie is off today with shingles and I'm stuck on the till.

(GARY leaves the stage, stealthily. DARYL looks up again.)

DARYL	Woah!! Did you see that?

(As DOUG stands beside him, gaping up at the skylight, unbeknown to DOUG, DARYL takes a huge greedy bite out of DOUG's frosted doughnut. DOUG, catches him, shrugs and laughs.)

DARYL	*(chewing)* Mind if I sit down? That psycho mate of yours has been riding me all morning.
DOUG	*(chuckles)* Sure. Knock yourself out.
DARYL	So how do you know, Rambo?
DOUG	Gary? We were in the Special Forces together.
DARYL	You were in the Special Forces? You look like an accountant.

DOUG   What?? Me!? Now, that's an irony. *(DOUG chuckles to himself.)*

DARYL   What did I say?

        (Sound of gunshots offstage)

DARYL   Do you think...?

        (Pregnant pause.)

DOUG   Car backfiring.

DARYL   You sure?

DOUG   Once you've been in the services you can always tell.

DARYL   So tell me, why is it an 'irony'?

DOUG   I shouldn't say. He'll get pissed off with me.

DARYL   Come on. What?

DOUG   Well, I probably shouldn't say...

DARYL   Go on...

DOUG   Well...Gary is the accountant.

DARYL   What? I thought you were both in the Special Forces.

DOUG   We were. Fully trained commandos. But Gary was in admin.

DARYL   Admin??

DOUG   Sure. The commandos has an admin like every other division of the army. I was a sapper. But Gaz was in accounts. Mostly did our pays and tax returns. Good with numbers, Gary. Bit bitter about it, though. In Afghanistan we were out on special ops while Gaz was mostly in HQ doing the battalion's taxes.

        (DARYL detonates with laughter. DOUG reluctantly joins in. We hear a buzz on the intercom. (drying his eyes) Hey!

Don't tell him I told you. This is the first job he's had since leaving the army. He'll never speak to me again.

(We hear a buzz on the intercom).

GARY   *(Off stage)* Buzzards fly west in June.

DOUG   *(pressing button)* But often fly east in May.

DARYL   Buzzards add ten percent for GST every fiscal quarter.

(DOUG shushes him).

GARY   *(Offstage)* Squawk.

DOUG   Squawk.

DARYL   Squawk.

(GARY returns.)

GARY   Nothin! A layer of dust on the roof but no footprints.

DARYL   Must have been a buzzard.

GARY   There's no buzzards around here. Haaang on...!

(GARY walks up to DARYL, who has a snow ring of frosted sugar around his mouth. GARY drags his fingers over DARYL's lips before tasting his fingers.)

GARY   *(to DOUG)* You haven't been feeding our little bird, have you Douglas?

(DOUG looks at his doughnut and frowns.)

DOUG   He must have snatched a bite when I was looking up at the skylight. In fact, that's probably...

GARY   Get on that bike, Lard Arse. You got an extra kilo to burn.

DARYL   I'm bloody starving! (to DOUG) Rambo's starving me. Anyway, it was worth it. I'd sell my first born for a bag of donuts.

GARY	You won't be saying that in an hour.
DOUG	*(shaking his head, chuckling)* I'd better push off.
	(GARY leaves the stage with his kit.)
DARYL	Tell me, why did you leave the army to work in an electronics store?
DOUG	*(mysterious look)* Gary knows. *(DOUG exits the stage finishing the rest of his doughnut before poking his head on stage again.)*
DOUG	Hey, remember. Mum's the word about the accountancy stuff.
	(DARYL salutes. GARY enters without the combat gear.)
GARY	Keep pedalling. You've got a long way to go, soldier.
DARYL	So your mate Doug? Was he a good soldier?
GARY	He was someone I could rely on in a jam.
DARYL	Photocopier jam?
GARY	What?
	(We hear a buzz on the intercom.)
GARY	*(into intercom)* Who is it?
SHONA	*(offstage)* Me. Let me in.
GARY	Buzzards fly west in June.
SHONA	*(offstage)* I can't remember your bloody codes, Gary. It's Shona. Just let me in, will you?
GARY	I repeat. Buzzards fly west in June!
SHONA	*(offstage)* Gary. I'm tired. I'm depressed. I'm premenstrual. I can't remember your stupid codes. I need you to let me in. I've drunk four coffees this morning. I'm desperate for a piss.

DARYL	(*smirking*) Sounds like a trap to me, Gary.
GARY	(*nodding*) Exactly what I'm thinking.
DARYL	(*salutes*) No flies on you, soldier.
GARY	You better believe it. (*into intercom*) I repeat. I repeat. Buzzards fly west in June. Buzzards fly west in June.
SHONA	(*offstage*) GARY! OPEN THE FUCKING DOOR BEFORE I PISS MYSELF OR I'M GOING TO KILL YOU!

(*GARY quickly buzzes her in.*)

DARYL	Weak as piss.
GARY	You don't know what she's like when she's in a bad mood.
DARYL	Imagine she's the Taliban with an AK 47. Use your imagination.
GARY	When she comes back from the loo you'll see what I mean.
DARYL	You sure you were in the Special Forces? Or was it H and R Block?

(*GARY shoots him a worried look.*)

I know...keep pedalling, Maggot.

(*SHONA enters doing up the belt of her combat trousers*).

SHONA	What is it with you?? I just about pissed myself in the street, fool. Why didn't you buzz me up? You do that again and I'll kick you square in the balls, Gary Dooley.
GARY	Shona, we agreed on codes. You are always saying keep it professional.
SHONA	No. You agreed on codes, Gary. I think my answer was "yeah, whatever, just don't forget the bloody pizzas".
GARY	We all agreed. Kevin uses them without a problem.

SHONA   That's because Kevin has no life.

DARYL   Professionalism?

GARY/SHONA   Shut up and pedal!

GARY   In special forces I never went anywhere without my code
                 book.

DARYL   Or a calculator.

GARY   Any soldier not knowing the right codes could find himself...

DARYL   ...Or herself! Tell him, Shona! Women are in the front line
                 now.

GARY   ... or herself, shot!

DARYL   Or without a tax return.

SHONA   What is he banging on about taxes for?

DARYL   *(smiling to himself)* Oh...something Doug told me.

                 (GARY looks horrified.)

SHONA   Doug? DOUG?? You haven't let a member of the public in
                 here, Gary? That is something we all agreed not to do.

GARY   He's not any member of the public. He's ex-job. We were in
                 Afghanistan together. He's someone I can rely on.

DARYL   Doug armed with an M16. Gary with an Excel Spreadsheet.

SHONA   Oh, I've left my purse in the loo. Back in a minute.

                 *(SHONA leaves. GARY races over to DARYL on the
                 exercise machine, panicked.)*

GARY   Okay, so you know. Congratulations. But if you let on about
                 it, I can make life very difficult for you in here.

DARYL   As opposed to the life of luxury I'm leading now? As far as
                 I'm concerned I've got nothing to lose. When Shona walks

in, I'm telling her that the only way you would kill a Taliban terrorist is if he defaulted on his tax returns.

(SHONA returns. GARY paces.)

SHONA   Gary, I need you to cover for me for another two hours. I have some banking to do.

DARYL   Shona, from now on you should let Gary do all the banking and accounts. I need to tell you something about him...

(GARY holds his breath.)

SHONA   What?

DARYL   He's a training psycho. I'm spent. My 'get up and go' has 'got up and gone'.

SHONA   Gary?

GARY   Eh...yeah, I've worked him pretty hard this morning.

SHONA   I'm off. When I come back, no codes. Right?

GARY   But we agreed on the codes, Shona.

(DARYL hops off the bike and walks around to SHONA's handbag and secretly lifts her mobile phone.)

SHONA   *(sighs)* Okay. Okay. Christ! What is it again?

GARY   "Buzzards fly west in June".

SHONA   Why does it have to be buzzards? It's very American. Why can't it be something British like a robins or chickens?

GARY   Chickens?

SHONA   Why not?

DARYL   *(from the lounge area, eating a rice cake)* Chickens don't fly. They just run about like lunatics trying to pinch your chips. Or in my case, rice crackers.

GARY	Cos buzzards sounds cool. You know, like a film.
SHONA	So you can't be cool if you use British fauna?
GARY	Now you want to use flowers?
SHONA	*(losing her patience)* Look, if I ring from downstairs, just bloody let me in! Okay?
GARY	Okay. Okay. "Chickens fly west in June" it is.
DARYL	But do they fly at all?
SHONA	Will you shut up! I don't need you butting in all the time making things worse. *(to GARY)* Okay. Chickens it is. Goodbye.
GARY	But what about the countersign?
SHONA	For Christ's sake?!!
GARY	"But often fly east in May". Then I say "squawk". And then you say "squawk".
SHONA	*(sotto voce)* God, kill me now. *(to GARY)* Okay, I got it. "Squawk". Bye.
DARYL	But chickens don't squawk…they cluck.
SHONA	Will you shut up!
	(SHONA leaves. GARY paces.)
GARY	I've got to have a smoke. My nerves can't take much more of this. Can I trust you or do I have to cuff you to the sink?
DARYL	What am I going to do to against an ex-Special Forces trained accountant?
	(GARY's shoulders drop and he leaves. DARYL quickly pulls out the phone from the hiding spot. He puts it on loudspeaker and dials.)

DARYL	*(to self)* God, this phone is one of those stupid Mulberries or whatever they're called. How do I dial? How do I DIAL ?? I know!! I know! The last number dialed.
	(We hear the phone dial on loudspeaker.)
CHAN	*(offstage)* Hello, Chan's Chinese Malaysian takeaway. Can I have your telephone number and address thanking you?
DARYL	I don't know the number or the address but…
CHAN	Must have your address for quick and prompt delivery thanking you.
DARYL	You don't understand. I'm being held against my will I need you to…
	(We hear another phone ring in the background. CHAN screams something in Cantonese to another member of staff.)
CHAN	Sorry. Can I have your address please thanking you?
DARYL	Look, you don't understand! I don't have much time. He's a trained psycho accountant. I must do this quickly…
CHAN	No worry. We very quick. Delivery only twenty minutes thanking you.
DARYL	No, no. I don't care about that. I…
CHAN	You wan pick up, instead? Free prawn rice this month.
	(We hear someone shouting something at him in Cantonese. CHAN shouts back, furiously.)
CHAN	Computer say this Shona's phone. You want the usual? 15, 23 and 28 with cashews but not too spicy thanking you?
	(DARYL hears footsteps up the stairs.)

DARYL	Whatever! Whatever! I've got to go!
	(DARYL hangs up and hides the phone in the back of his underpants. GARY enters, pacing.)
GARY	I've been thinking. Why didn't you give me up to Shona. I don't get it.
DARYL	What's the point? I'd still be here eating rice crackers and celery sticks. I mean, you trained with them and everything. You were actually in the Special Forces, right?
GARY	Trained just as hard as anyone did. Harder. It's just, well... administration doesn't quite have the glamour as the front line boys. I'd hate to lose face with Shona and Kevin. I'd appreciate it if you didn't say anything...
DARYL	Your secret's safe with me, Rambo.
GARY	Just for that I'm going to give you an extra ration of crackers tonight!
DARYL	*(dryly)* Generous. Tell me. Why did you and your pal leave the army, anyway? Sounds like it's shrouded in mystery.
GARY	Long story.
DARYL	I'm not going anywhere in case you haven't noticed.
GARY	I've signed the Official Secrets Act.
DARYL	God, Gary that sounds like one of those tedious codes of yours. Wouldn't you feel better getting it off your chest?
GARY	I can't.
DARYL	You'd feel better. Cleansed. You know, I never told you this but I was in the army when I was young.
GARY	Bullshit.

DARYL	Okay. Cadets. And I bloody hated it. Some idiot yelling in my face after school. Could get that at home from dad for free.

(GARY laughs.)

GARY	Ok, I'll tell ya. But if you tell anyone about this I'll hunt you down and kill you in your sleep. And you know I will.
DARYL	But not before the end of the fiscal year.

(GARY deflates)

DARYL	So start at the beginning.

(Lights dim. GARY is picked up by a spotlight).

GARY	If you've never been to Afghanistan you're not missing much. It's a dusty shithole of a place. I was mostly in HQ doing the books. Doug's told you probably. It was mundane. You fall into a routine. So you notice unusual things when they pop up. I found I kept having to sign off on funds for a special op called - well I can't tell you what it was called because that would be contravening the act - but it was very *(taps his nose)* hush hush. Anyway, I can see where it's taking place simply from where the weekly rations are being sent. So I make me way over there. I take Dougy with me for backup. Anyways, we weave through stinking backstreets and eventually find the safe-house. We make our way inside. Joint's empty. Then we hear muffled noises. Dougy and me make our way to the basement and find a locked door. We force it open. The room's dark and smells of shit. Human shit. And inside, strapped to a chair, is this little local Arab bloke with a hood over his face. Naked. We walk over to him he's trembling. We lift the hood and it's

just a kid. Maybe fourteen years old. Dunno. The look in his eyes was sumthun I'll never forget. I've seen blokes scared before. But this... He started crying. Like a little boy. Asking for his mother. I speak a little street Arabic. We all do. Part of the training, an that. So I calm the kid. Tell him I'll be back. We come back the next day but he's gone. Tried to find out what happened. Went to me superiors, an that. Told em what I'd seen. They said it was an American special op and I was to say nuthin about it. Three months later, Doug and me receive a letter from divisional HQ saying the unit is undergoing cost cutting and we're asked to take redundancy. Funny how it was just us two blokes. Out of an entire unit. Me and Doug. Then we were offered a big chunk of moola, our civvies and shown the door. Doug used his cash to buy the electronics store.

DARYL   *(quietly)* What did you use your cash for?

GARY   Getting pissed. Gambling. If I'd invested it I wouldn't be training you miserable fat pricks all day, that's for sure.

DARYL   So why are you doing this if you hate it so much?

GARY   You don't understand. The army was me entire world. I can't explain it but it's...like a cult. You live it, you sleep it, you breathe it. You dream in camouflage.

DARYL   I dream in butter.

GARY   When I found that room in Afghanistan...it shook me entire world. Me faith in everything I believed in. That was wrong.

DARYL   *(exacerbated)* Gary, haven't you learned anything from that experience?? Haven't you learned that keeping people against their will without trial - or in my case, to lose a few pounds…

GARY   A few?

DARYL   Ok, more than a few. But that it is fundamentally wrong?
Or are you looking for some sort of reckoning?

(GARY looks away.)

That's it! You're doing this to somehow reconcile your soul.
You don't see me. You see that kid in Afghanistan. You see
the part you played in it by proxy. The part we all play in it,
in our plasma-screened complicity. The whole dirty business.
Kidnapping me is reconciling your soul.

GARY   Enough talk. I need a drink. Might head to the pub.

DARYL   Can you at least bring me back a nice cold one?

GARY   Beer? You're kidding, right?

DARYL   Okay. How about some low carb lager?

GARY   Against the rules, soldier.

DARYL   Rules? Rules?? Holding a grown man hostage and starving
him half to death because his wife says he's too fat is against
the rules, too! What do the rules mean anymore, Gary? You
were part of a system that was all about rules and
regulations. People bend rules to suit their own purpose.

GARY   Dunno. You'll have to work it off tomorrow. Game might
not be worth the candle. You up for it, Daryl? It'll be tough.

DARYL   (hugs him) That's the first time you've used my real name.

(GARY sneers.)

DARYL   (salutes) I will work my big fat butt off tomorrow, sir.

GARY   Not sure.

DARYL   Okay, how about this? We go to the pub, sink a few beers, chat about Afghanistan. Get some things off your chest.

GARY   *(laughing)* Haaang on! The others might be stupid. But I'm not. I'm not taking you to any pub, club or fast food outlet. In fact, I'm not taking you out of this room, pal. I'll bring back a six pack of low carb for us to share but that's it. Shona would have my guts for garters just for that alone.

DARYL   Three beers? Won't even touch the sides, mate.

GARY   Yeah, and you've got plenty to touch, Daryl. But actually...I'm not supposed to leave you for more than five minutes. So on second thoughts, I might have to forget it.

DARYL   Gary! Mate! You can't do this to me! You can't dangle a beer over someone and then take it away. That's called assault in South London.

GARY   Not supposed to leave the perimeter.

DARYL   Then handcuff me to the sink.

GARY   Nah. Have to think of health and safety.

DARYL   You're quoting health and safety at me after bundling me in the boot of a car??

GARY   That boot is fitted with cameras, listening devices, devices to measure your heart rate. The lot. We're not some Mickey Mouse operation here.

DARYL   Okay. What would you do to an enemy prisoner?

GARY   Hood. Handcuffs. Fetters. Naked.

DARYL   The Gitmo package, eh? Okay. For a beer. I'll do it.

GARY   Actually, I've left the hood and cuffs at home.

DARYL   Okay. How about this? You take all my clothes. Lock me in.

What can I do naked and locked in? Secure...vulnerable...

(GARY mulls this over)

GARY   I don't know. Shona would be furious if anything went wrong.

DARYL   What could go wrong? This is for beer, remember? BEER! That blessed 'support group' in a bottle. That little liquid happiness. Look, it will be strictly between former soldiers.

GARY   I don't know...

DARYL   Did I tell Shona about you being a highly trained lethal accountant? Gary, I'm gasping for a beer. You're a bloke. You know how it is, surely!

GARY   *(nodding)* True.

DARYL   *(drops his pants)* You've got to learn to trust people, Gary.

            ('Stealth music. SEE PAGE 91)

BLACKOUT.

END OF SCENE 1.

ACT 2
SCENE 2 MIND CONTROL AND SELF DISCIPLINE

The audience are in darkness and the stage is also in darkness. SHONA, KEVIN and GARY are heard in the darkness as they flash torches at the audience in their seats. (The actors can have fun with this, improvising with the audience. e.g. "Shona, I hear a fattie breathing in the dark over here." Gary says "this is what happens when you trust fat people. They're scheming bastards.")

Suddenly, a follow-spot picks up DARYL, in front of the stage curtain. He is stark naked, holding a small terracotta pot over his genitals. SHONA blows a whistle. DARYL bolts off-stage like a startled rabbit. The cast shout and give chase upon seeing him. The actors leave the audience in darkness. We hear GARY yell "Gotcha piggy!!" In the dark we hear tranquil eastern meditation music until the stage lights are raised. We find KEVIN and DARYL sitting in the lotus position on two large cushions. KEVIN is dressed like a Buddhist Monk. DARYL, trademark lumberjack shirt and jeans, has a garland of flowers around his head. They both speak to each other with their eyes closed. The calendar reveals it's two weeks later.

KEVIN	*(eyes closed)* The only way you will maintain your goal body-weight after you leave us is by using positive visualization.
DARYL	*(eyes closed)* I think it's working.
KEVIN	Great! Great!! What are you seeing right now?
DARYL	A McValue Meal.
KEVIN	*(sighs, eyes still closed)* Ok. Well, thanks for being honest, at least. That's perfectly understandable. Now I want you to

	see that McValue Meal float away down a long river. Can you see that? Can you see that?
DARYL	Yes. I can see it.
KEVIN	Excellent. Excellent. What are you seeing right now?
DARYL	*(eyes closed)* A fat bloke in a lumberjack shirt swimming after it.
KEVIN	*(controlling anger)* Work with me, Daryl. Work with me. Ok. Keep that image. I want you to swim after the McValue Meal and sink it. Send it to the bottom of the river. Can you do that?
DARYL	Yep, I'm sinking it.
	(DARYL opens one eye to peak at KEVIN. He gets up quietly and tiptoes to the door, swiping KEVIN's pass.)
KEVIN	What are you seeing now, Daryl?
	(DARYL quietly opens the door only to find GARY standing there holding a large club, tapping it in his hand.)
DARYL	*(dryly, from the door)* Club sandwich.
KEVIN	*(peeking with one eye)* Do you want it?
DARYL	Not particularly.
	(DARYL gives the finger to GARY. Closes the door and resumes his trance. Both KEVIN and DARYL have their eyes shut.)
KEVIN	Good. Now just breeeeathe.
	(They both take long, deep breaths.)
DARYL	*(opens his eyes)* You're a Buddhist, right?
KEVIN	I want you to hold that river image in your mind. This time

in a positive sense. Make it work for you.

DARYL   Ever seen a picture of him? The Buddha?

KEVIN   Now, I want you to imagine the river as your blood. But
            instead of being murky and turbid, it's clean and healthy!

DARYL   That's why they call him the Laughing Buddha. Because he's
            just so happy being fat. He's a fat, happy, bloke.

KEVIN   And that river is flowing, full of life.

DARYL   You see, I think you're missing the core essence of
            Buddhism.

KEVIN   *(exploding)* Buddhism is about moderation.! Self control!
            Awareness, Daryl! That's what I'm trying to share with you!!

DARYL   It's about fat blokes being happy.

KEVIN   *(controlling himself)* Work with me, Daryl. Take some deep
            breaths. Clear your mind.

            (DARYL takes some yoga style breaths.)

KEVIN   Just concentrate on your breath. How do you feel?

DARYL   Like a beer.

KEVIN   *(opening his eyes)* This is hopeless! *(KEVIN gets up and
            presses 'stop' on the CD player. MUSIC stops.)*

KEVIN   *(shouting)* This is only going to work if you take it seriously,
            Daryl!

            (We hear a buzz on the intercom.)

KEVIN   *(into intercom)* Shona?

CHAN   *(Offstage over intercom)* Chan's Chinese Malaysian take-
            away. Have your order here. Going cold thanking you.

KEVIN   I didn't order any food, Chan. I don't understand.

CHAN   *(Offstage)* Have your order here thanking you.

KEVIN   There must be some kind of mistake again, Chan. I didn't order any food. I don't know why this keeps occurring.

CHAN   You call me three times this week and order food only to cancel order. I call the police now. You fucking racists! I know where you people live, remember. I call the police now!

                (DARYL rushes for the intercom.)

DARYL   You call them, Chan. Don't let these racists make a fool of you.

                (KEVIN pushes him away.)

KEVIN   Please don't do that, Chan. Just leave the food with Gary. *(to DARYL)* I don't understand, that's the third time this week. I'm putting on a few unwanted pounds with all this Chinese food.

DARYL   Buddha would be proud.

                (GARY appears with the food.)

KEVIN   Did you order this?

GARY   No. I don't eat this oily shit. *(pointing at DARYL)* That's what they eat. The fatties.

DARYL   No, you choose the healthy diet: Marlborough Light.

GARY   I figured you ordered it. Must be Shona.

                (Suddenly DARYL's pocket rings. KEVIN and GARY look shocked. GARY pins DARYL and wrestles the mobile from him. KEVIN answers it.)

KEVIN   *(into phone)* Shona is that you? No, no, no. Hang on. It's not a Practical joke. Daryl must have swiped your phone. Yes, I'll tell him.

DARYL	Tell her mobile phones give you brain tumours.
KEVIN	Yes, I'll tell him, Shona.
DARYL	And that's how I want you all to go.
KEVIN	Yes, I'll tell him.
	(KEVIN takes out a steel box and locks SHONA's phone in it.)
GARY	The sly bastard. That's what all this Chinese food has been about all week. He's been calling them all along. *(to DARYL)* I don't get it. Why didn't you just call the police?
DARYL	The police?? THE POLICE??? Because the bloody thing's locked! That's why!! All I could do was dial the last number called. Do you think I could get that bloody Chan to help me? All I got out of him were free prawn crackers.
GARY	Shona's been back to every cafe in the area trying to find it. I'll call her from the caravan and explain what's been going on. She might need to go and see Chan and explain.
	(GARY leaves.)
DARYL	*(incredulous, shouting after GARY)* Yes, do tell him that it wasn't Shona but the hostage you are holding, starving and torturing. Your hostage is selfish like that. Always thinking of himself.
KEVIN	*(furious)* All this is for you, Daryl. When will you realise that?
DARYL	For me?? What a joke! You don't care about me. You just want the money. Let's face it.
KEVIN	That's not true. We are doing this because we are committed to helping people.

DARYL	And Gary?
KEVIN	*(quietly)* Well, he has his reasons.
DARYL	You're naive, Kev. Really, you are. Too much bottled water.
KEVIN	I'm naive? Have you looked in the mirror, lately?? You look pretty darn good, Daryl. Have a peek.
	(KEVIN drags DARYL to the mirror.)
DARYL	*(checking himself out)* Yeah, I've lost a few pounds, I guess. So what? Now I need to buy new threads. More bloody shopping. What a drag!
KEVIN	Well, at least you won't need to hide behind oversized lumberjack shirts, anymore. I know! You can have a lumberjack shirt burn-off at the reveal. That would be a lot of fun. Kinda symbolic.
DARYL	*(to KEVIN)* Hey, what's wrong with lumberjack shirts?
KEVIN	Pul-ease!
DARYL	It's my look.
KEVIN	You don't actually believe that, do you?
DARYL	Of course.
KEVIN	Daryl, when we are overweight, we develop 'a look' to avoid people taking our bodies seriously. Taking us seriously.
DARYL	What a load of crap.
	(DARYL sneaks a spring roll from the Chinese food).
KEVIN	True. I know. I used to wear oversized novelty T-shirts that would make people laugh. The archetypal jolly fat man.

DARYL	I am jolly. I am fat. And I'm fine with it.
KEVIN	*(angry)* Face facts. You're fat and depressed and hiding behind a look that went out in the late 80s.
DARYL	*(angry)* Hey! Lumberjack shirts are back! Hipsters are wearing them. Bernice read it in the Evening Standard.
KEVIN	*(yelling)* Skinny suits and ties are back, Daryl. What would you look like in a skinny suit?
DARYL	*(angry)* Like a knob! You know what they say, "if you've lived through a fashion, you're too old to wear it again".
KEVIN	What about the lumberjack shirts, then?
DARYL	Ahh-ah! You see, I never stopped wearing them. That's always been my look. Since uni.
KEVIN	You went to uni?
DARYL	Studied Oriental Philosophy.
KEVIN	Wow! Really? Then why are you selling soft drinks in South London?
DARYL	It's very simple. In my first week at Bristol University, I was on the bog in the student toilets. Above the toilet roll were these salient words: Philosophy Degree. Please take one.

(KEVIN moves the Chinese food on the table.)

KEVIN	You're a dark horse, Daryl. And here I am teaching you Zen.
DARYL	That's why you can trust me. I believe in karma.
KEVIN	So if I leave this very fattening Chinese food here while I nip to the loo, you won't eat it because you know the person you'll be most letting down is yourself.
DARYL	Exactly. Leave all the food here. I don't need the bad karma.

KEVIN   Now, if I come back and catch you eating all the Chinese I'll be disappointed in you. It will be bad karma. Not only spiritually but physically. Karma is a metaphor. You'll be back at last week's weight and you won't leave here early as planned. If you break my trust again, you'll feel terrible. Remember last time. The vegetable oil? You felt awful, all week.

DARYL   You're right. I would feel bad. But you can trust me.

                     (KEVIN leaves.)

DARYL   *(to himself)* I feel terrible, Kevin. I really do. But last week my karma ran over my dogma. Now, where's the chilli sauce?

                     (DARYL devours the food. Blackout. In the darkness we hear Eric Idle's 'I like Chinese'.)

END OF SCENE 2

ACT 2

SCENE 3 TEMPTATION ROOM

Lights are raised. The calendar reveals it is a week later. The table has been transformed into a fat man's paradise: cakes, hamburgers, pies, creamy doughnuts, the works! KEVIN and GARY lead DARYL back onto set with a hood. SHONA follows. GARY removes the hood and leaves.

DARYL   Holy kilojoule! It's like a dream.

KEVIN   This is an exercise in temptation, Daryl. You let me down last week with the Chinese food but who did you really let down?

DARYL   Myself, Kevin. I feel bad about it. I really do.

KEVIN   I know you do, Daryl. But in this exercise you are allowed one item from this fatty selection. Because in the outside world you will be expected to have a treat every now and then but you need to find the willpower to stop. This is where obese people let themselves down – willpower.

DARYL   I'm not obese but fat and contented. Remember?

KEVIN   According to the BMI you are still obese, Daryl.

DARYL   I always go off the FCI. More of a British Standard.

KEVIN   The FCI? I've not heard of it.

DARYL   The Fishing Club Index. Compared to the blokes in my local fishing club, I'm bordering on anorexic.

KEVIN   Now, you must pick one item. And one item only. Can we trust you?

DARYL   Need you ask?

(KEVIN and SHONA leave the stage. SHONA brings her fingers to her eyes then at DARYL as if to say "I'm watching you". Blackout. In the darkness we hear Lionel Bart's 'Food Glorious Food' - from the musical Oliver! as the set is modified by stage hands. Lights are raised and we see that the plates and cake stands are almost empty. DARYL has eaten most of it and a lot of it is on his face and in his hair. SHONA and KEVIN return, shocked.)

SHONA   What on earth...? You were supposed to eat one thing and one thing only! How could you eat so much food in ten minutes?

DARYL   *(yelling)* I'm from South London! These are the ways of my people!

SHONA   *(yelling)* Well, "your people" must be morbidly obese!

DARYL   It's all to do with living through World War Two. A Londoner's philosophy is – if it's there – eat it before they ration it. Why do you think there are so many restaurants in London? We're all terrified the Government's going to bring back rationing in the next Budget!

KEVIN   *(to SHONA)* And I thought we were getting somewhere with the meditation techniques. He's beyond hopeless! What is the point??

SHONA   *(throwing food at DARYL)* I don't get you, Daryl. It's like you are happy being fat!

DARYL   *(claps)* At last! Give the lady a cigar! I AM HAPPY BEING FAT. I don't care that I look 'chunky' in a lumberjack shirt. I don't care if my wife's run off with her Pilates instructor. He can have her. I like being me–Fat. Happy. Daryl.

SHONA   Daryl, we've told you for weeks. We don't believe your wife has done this to you and run off with her Pilates instructor. No one does that. That's using Feedem Fighters in a really shitty way. No one is really that vindictive.

KEVIN   Besides, you've lied about everything. You told Shona you had a degree in English Literature. You told me you have a degree in Eastern Philosophy. You told Gary you were in the army.

DARYL   *(slyly, eating the food)* I said I studied Eastern Philosophy - which I did before switching to English Lit - or if you like, from one bog roll to another. I told Gary I was in the cadets. It's the truth when I say my wife has done this to set me up. Why won't you believe me??

SHONA   Well, who'd blame her, frankly. We've had you here for eight weeks and frankly, we are sick to death of you.

DARYL   *(eating)* Not true. Deep down you like me, Shona. Don't deny it.

(She rolls her eyes.)

KEVIN   Well, you make me frustrated, I don't mind telling you.

DARYL   *(eating)* Then let me go. Easy as.

SHONA   Daryl, no matter how many times we tell you. You don't seem to get it. We have two signed contracts. You have ten lousy pounds to go - twenty now you've had an orgy in the temptation room - so why don't you just work really hard for a week and lose the ten pounds and do us all a favour and PISS OFF?

DARYL   *(surprised)* Is that all I have to lose? Ten pounds? You're kidding?

SHONA   Before today, well...yes.

DARYL	*(Putting down donut)* Are you telling me I've lost the entire goal weight?
SHONA	Well...almost, yes.
DARYL	*(to KEVIN)* You know...I bet she thought I'd never do it.
KEVIN	Shona?
DARYL	No. Bernice. I bet she thought, "I'll sign the early release clause, sure. Why not? The fat prick has no willpower. He'll never do it." Hey, I know! Maybe I'll fly to the Italian Riviera and surprise them. Lounge at the pool in some tight trunks.
KEVIN	That's the spirit!
DARYL	I've just got to find some willpower.
	(DARYL punches his chest, salutes Black Panther style, shouting 'WILL POWER')
KEVIN	At last! That's what I'm trying to teach you. Self discipline, Daryl. Willpower.
DARYL	Okay. I've just got to get tough with myself. I want you to put a bottle of beer in front of me. I'll prove it to you.
	(KEVIN exits and returns with the bottle of beer.)
DARYL	Go on. Open it and leave it on the table.
	(SHONA opens it and leaves it on the table. They stand back and watch. DARYL grabs the bottle and starts chugging it down.)
SHONA	Kevin! Kevin!! Grab that bottle off him! It's a bloody trick! If he puts on more weight, we'll never be rid of him!!

(KEVIN chases DARYL around the stage as he tries to drink it as DARYL shouts "Willpower! Willpower!")

BLACKOUT.

END OF SCENE 3.

FEEDEM FIGHTERS
ACT 3
SCENE 1 DANCING CLASS

We hear hip hop music. DARYL, headband, shorts and thongs, is being put through his paces by PARIS, a camp dance instructor. PARIS dances,

SHONA reads a novel, seated.

PARIS	Come on! Lift those gorgeous legs, Daryl! Let's get down with the beat. Dancing is a great fun way to stay trim.
	(DARYL is beyond hopeless. He is hardly trying. PARIS stops the music in a huff.)
PARIS	*(folding his arms)* You're not putting your heart into it, Daz.
DARYL	That's because my heart's not in it, Paris. Is that your real name? Paris? As in that fool who started the Trojan War?
	(SHONA lifts her head from her book.)
PARIS	Yes, my parents met in France. I was conceived there.
DARYL	Using that logic I should change my name to 'Tooting'.
PARIS	Have you ever actually danced before?
DARYL	Only at weddings between food courses.
PARIS	Shame.
DARYL	Yeah, Bernice hates dancing. Well, she hates dancing with me. Says I dance like I'm stubbing out cigarettes butts. *(shows them a crude twist move)* She usually finds someone else to dance with while I head to the buffet sourcing posh food.

PARIS	So you eat to cope with depression?
DARYL	*(exasperated)* No, I eat because I like food! Is there anything wrong with liking food? Here we all are obsessed with MasterChef and every possible kind of cooking show known to man, while at the same time feeling guilty about eating! No wonder we're all on the edge of a nervous breakdown. I. Like. Food!!
PARIS	Let's try something a little slower.
DARYL	Sounds more my style.
PARIS	Ever tangoed?
	(DARYL shrugs.)
PARIS	Shona, Daryl needs a dance partner. Pop up here, darling.
DARYL	She doesn't like it when you call her 'darling'. Says it's patronising to women.
SHONA	*(from the couch)* I'm not a dancer, I'm afraid, Paris. Another time.
DARYL	Shona's the intellectual type, aren't you? Hard core socialist at uni who after the fall of communism fell into a political black hole that she's been trying to dig her way out of ever since.
SHONA	*(head in book)* You're mixing your metaphors, Daryl.
DARYL	She satisfies those undergraduate urges by kidnapping unsuspecting fatties, while all the time thinking she's fighting for the Sandanistas and defeating American Imperialism with low fat alternatives.
SHONA	*(reading, smiling)* I'll be glad when we have fulfilled our contract and we can see the back of you Daryl Lucas.

DARYL   She doesn't mean that, Paris. You see, she's grown rather fond of me. Each day she falls a little deeper for me. Leaves me with junk food disguised as 'trust exercises' so I'll pig out and never leave. That way she can keep her bird in its cage for a few more precious weeks.

(SHONA chuckles, shaking her head.)

DARYL   She'll miss me when I go. She's secretly in love with me.

SHONA   I can't wait till you leave. Believe me.

DARYL   Well, you better drag your toosh over here and dance with me.

PARIS   Come on, Shona. You need to inspire your clients, darling.

DARYL   Huh! Is that what I am? A client? Victim more like it.

(SHONA puts down her book and limps over begrudgingly.)

SHONA   *(sighs)* Okay. What do I have to do?

PARIS   Put your arm around his neck and take his hand in yours.

(SHONA does. PARIS hits the tango music on a portable CD player on stage - this cues tango music. Suddenly DARYL snaps SHONA close and tangos like an Argentinian on caffeine tablets. He's amazing, turning her, dipping her. He is beyond dazzling. PARIS is open-mouthed with shock, whooping and hollering with each move. The dance is intimate, romantic, intense. As the music ends, PARIS applauds theatrically. SHONA flushes.)

SHONA   *(panting)* Where did you learn to dance like that?

DARYL   Oh, I'm full of surprises, Shona.

PARIS   *(clapping wildly)* Come on, Daz. Do tell, sweetie. Do tell.

DARYL   *(flatly)* Larry's Latin Dancing for Lovers. Course at

Battersea Arts Centre.

PARIS   God, I know, Larry! We worked together at the Ballet
Rambert years ago! I'd heard he moved up to God's
Waiting Room. So he opened a studio, eh? The sly old bitch.

DARYL   Thought I would surprise Bernice for her 40th. Like I said,
she always hated my dancing.

SHONA   Bet she was bowled over!

DARYL   *(sighing)* She was. Completely. Found her spread-eagled on
the floor with Christopher when I came home from work
one afternoon to surprise her for her birthday and take her
Latin dancing.

SHONA   *(quietly)* I'm sorry, Daryl. That's terrible.

DARYL   Put a dent in the evening's plans.

SHONA   Did you confront her?

DARYL   No point. They didn't see me. Too engrossed at the time to
notice a minor earthquake. So I went and sat in my car and
cried. Once I had my pity party, I plotted my escape. That is,
until she found the email to Di and I ended up here.

PARIS   *(packing up)* I better push off, Shona. I have a class   at
seven. Just wait till I tell my samba ladies about this.
God! That was a shock, Daryl. A real shock. You mustn't do
that to an unsuspecting dance teacher! *(blows kisses)* Ciao,
Shona, darling. *(at the door, to DARYL)* Daryl, dancing the
tango like that you can officially call yourself a metrosexual.

DARYL   Mate, I've been married twenty years to a woman who
despises me. I'm what you call a 'get-no-sexual'.

*(SHONA returns to her book on the sofa. PARIS leaves
humming.)*

SHONA	*(from the sofa - reading)* Kevin wants you to make the mushroom risotto he showed you.
DARYL	Sure. Okay. Will you join me? Have you had dinner? *(DARYL lights two candles. He sets two plates.)*
SHONA	At Feedem Fighters the staff don't eat with the clients.
DARYL	Captives. Well, at least come and help me cook it. *(SHONA puts down her book and reluctantly ambles over. They both chop and chat.)*
DARYL	So what's your motivation in all this. I was right about you being the displaced socialist/anarchist, wasn't I?
SHONA	Yes and no.
DARYL	Can you pass the garlic? What do you mean? Yes and no?
SHONA	You're right. I was the archetypal undergrad anarchist at uni but that's not why I started Feedem Fighters.
DARYL	So why did you start this business? If you can call it that.
SHONA	Private reasons.
DARYL	Come on. We've tangoed. I've pressed your surprisingly perky udders against my flaccid manboobs. *(SHONA chuckles. She looks down at her breasts.)*
SHONA	They were once as big as beanbags. I used to be fatter than pre-Loser Kevin, would you believe?
DARYL	You? No way! I can pick a fatty a mile off. You don't fit the bill.
SHONA	You are right about that.
DARYL	What do you mean? Can you pass the cream cheese?
SHONA	Cream cheese??

DARYL   Wishful thinking. Anyway, what did you mean?

SHONA   *(waving him away)* Long story.

DARYL   I'm not going anywhere. I'm your hostage, remember?

SHONA   Client. You wouldn't be interested.

DARYL   Why not let me decide.

                 (SHONA gives a sigh.)

SHONA   Well, I guess I started putting on weight when I moved in with my last boyfriend. He was a merchant banker. So he was pretty cashed up. Always taking me to exotic restaurants. He loved fatty food. But he never put on weight for some reason.

DARYL   Can you pass me the fun-free-this-tastes-like-rubber-cheese?

                 (SHONA passes the cheese.)

SHONA   Anyway, I noticed I was putting on weight when none of my clothes fitted me anymore. This was strange. I'd never been heavy at school. At uni I was positively anorexic.

DARYL   Nothing worse than a fat anarchist.

SHONA   Agreed. Do you want me to chop the onions?

DARYL   No, I'll brave the onions. Haven't had a good cry since Westlife broke up. Go on.

SHONA   Well, I was getting fatter and fatter and fatter. I suggested we start to watch what we eat. Give the restaurants a miss for a while. But Connor - my defacto - was having none of it. He liked eating out. Said he liked me with a bit of a figure. Rubenesque. So I didn't worry about it, too much.It wasn't until my sister's wedding that I realised I was becoming obese. Couldn't fit into the bridesmaid's dress that was hanging off me only six months before. At this rate of weight-gain I'd need a crane to get me out of bed.

DARYL   So you put on a few pounds. Welcome to my world.

SHONA   Try 160 pounds in six months.

DARYL   160?? You must have been a real blimpo!

SHONA   I was. So I started to crash diet. But it was impossible. Connor kept taking me out and getting me pissed, forcing me to eat the fattiest dishes on the menu. I was getting fatter and fatter. Weird thing was, the bigger I got, the more he liked it. Maddening. It was like he was stuffing a goose.

DARYL   That's queer. Most of us like our girls at least skinnier than ourselves. In my case, that isn't hard.

SHONA   Hey, don't beat up on yourself. You've lost a lot of pounds, Daryl Lucas. Pass the mushrooms. You look pretty hot.

DARYL   Hot? No one's ever called me 'hot' before.

SHONA   (chopping) Anyway, it wasn't long after the wedding that I found the websites.

DARYL   (wincing) Young girls?

SHONA   No.

DARYL   What then?

SHONA   Morbidly obese women being shagged by skinny men. All the sites were the same. Disturbing. That's when I discovered Connor was a 'feeder'.

DARYL   A feeder?

SHONA   A 'feeder' is someone - usually a man - who gains sexual pleasure and psychological control from forcing another person to gain excessive weight.

DARYL	That's weird. Even for London.
SHONA	Even weirder if you are the goose being stuffed.
DARYL	So what did you do?
SHONA	I left him.
DARYL	Just like that?
SHONA	*(clicks her fingers)* Just like that. The day I found the websites, I moved out.
DARYL	Was it hard?
SHONA	Nope. Mum had a big house in Surrey. I owned a van. Easy.
DARYL	Did you have a job, then?
SHONA	No. But we'd been living together for ten years so I got quite a payout. Being a high profile merchant banker he couldn't have all the sordid details of our relationship coming out in court – or at least that's what my lawyer told his lawyer. So I took the money to start Feedem Fighters.
DARYL	So this job is personal.
SHONA	Like you wouldn't believe.
DARYL	Well, I like being fat. No one is forcing me to eat for sexual gratification. God, quite the contrary.
	(She laughs. They chop food in silence.)
DARYL	So? What did you think of my book?
SHONA	*(cooking)* What book?
DARYL	Get off! I know you read it. Don't deny it.
SHONA	*(chuckling)* You know, I thought you were lying about it, frankly.

DARYL	About writing a book?
SHONA	Well, yeah, sort of. It took me a while to find it. It was out almost on permanent loan at the library.
DARYL	So come on...what did you think?
SHONA	I have to admit. It's pretty funny, Daryl. You can certainly write. The characters were spot on. A good ear for dialogue.But the ending was a bit...
DARYL	Not very postmodern?
SHONA	Well...no. Not really. Bit corny.
DARYL	Sometimes life isn't very postmodern, Shona. Endings are just what they are: endings. Life's not one long literary device.
SHONA	So why sell soft drinks when you can write books? You sold a lot of books for a first-time novelist.
DARYL	Life happened.
SHONA	What do you mean?
DARYL	I met Bernice. It takes years to write a book. She wanted money now. She was never going to live in a garret from one measly royalty cheque to the next.
SHONA	Didn't she believe in you?
DARYL	Never even read the book.
SHONA	*(drops knife, open mouthed)* You are kidding??
DARYL	Nope. Never interested.
SHONA	*(chopping)* I don't believe you.
DARYL	An author can tell when someone has read his book.
SHONA	So why did you stay with her for 20 years?

DARYL   Laziness. I was trying to leave her when all this happened. When you lunatics arrived. She found my emails to Di at work.

SHONA   Ahh, so that's who she was talking about on the video when she said she 'found an email to Di.' Were you having an affair with this Di?

DARYL   God no! Di bats for the other side, if you follow my meaning.

            (SHONA scowls.)

DARYL   She was just talking me through it all. Our marriage was over, bar the shouting. I was trying to find a way out.

SHONA   So all this is true. She has done this to you with an alternative motive. You're sticking with that?

DARYL   I bet she's sunning herself by the pool at the Rapallo Grand right now.

SHONA   How do you know?

DARYL   Because that's where we had our honeymoon. She enjoys irony. I wanted to go to Florence, see the frescoes. But she insisted on Rapallo and cheap fags. I bet if you call she will be with our little 'ten-year-old son' Christopher, right now.

            (SHONA whips out her Blackberry and punches in numbers.)

DARYL   Shouldn't you have that locked in Kevin's vault?

SHONA   Mine has a lock, remember? Chan is still fuming about it.

DARYL   What are you doing?

SHONA   Googling the Rapallo Grand. *(She calls the number.)* Can I speak with Bernice…

DARYL	*(whispering)* Fisk! She'll use her maiden name. *(DARYL bites his bottom lip.)*
SHONA	Bernice Fisk please. *(pause)* Thanks. *(to DARYL)* Wow! They're connecting me. *(shrugs at DARYL)*
DARYL	Really? You're kidding??
SHONA	Bernice Fisk? Oh um Hi, I'm actually after Christopher. Is he there? No, he's not? He's in the bar. Right. No, no message. I do have the right Christopher? The Pilates instructor? Right. Good. No, it's ok. I'm just calling from the gym regarding classes and timetables for next term. It's not urgent. I'll email him next week. Bye.
	(SHONA hangs up. DARYL is shocked. He sits down and holds his head in his hands.)
SHONA	I don't understand. You said she'd be there and you were right. I actually believe you. You should feel vindicated.
DARYL	What's that line about life becoming a self-fulfilling prophesy? I guess part of me hoped it wouldn't be true.
	(SHONA sits beside him and puts her arm around him. Suddenly, he turns and they look into each other's eyes. DARYL leans to kiss. SHONA jumps up and paces the stage.)
SHONA	Daryl, I believe you about, Bernice. You don't need to do this. All this to try and make me let you go. I believe you.
DARYL	What would you say if I said I've fallen in love with you and you've fallen in love with me? Seriously??
SHONA	What!?? I'd say you are delirious and need junk food.
DARYL	How old are you? Late thirties?
SHONA	So?

DARYL   I'm forty. Newly single. Looking "hot" according to my
           dance partner. What say you and me make a go of it?

SHONA   You and me? I don't think so.

DARYL   Ahh, I get it now. You're the one with the trust issues. Not
           Kevin. It's you! Since the Merchant Feeder, what's-his-
           name...Connor. You no longer trust men. That's it!

SHONA   Rubbish.

DARYL   Well, you're going to end up a very lonely old woman,
           Shona. Love is all about taking a risk. Getting up and
           dusting yourself off and trying again, or so Di reckons. I'm
           up for it. Are you?

SHONA   If I found the right person.

DARYL   I *am* that person, Shona. Deep down you know it.

SHONA   But I'll never know, will I? I'll never know if this whole
           thing has been a trick to con me into letting you go.

           (DARYL thinks.)

DARYL   Okay. Then let me go. One week early. It's five lousy days.
           Big deal. I won't say anything to Bernice about Feedem
           Fighters letting me go early and breaking the contract. And
           I'll be here next week standing in that doorway in a tuxedo,
           with a dozen roses and two tickets to Italy.

SHONA   You must think I came down with the last shower. Nothing
           would convince me to let you go. Nothing.

DARYL   Not even this?

           *(He places a stick of celery in his mouth and does a mad
           Latin solo dance - making her laugh - before spitting out
           the celery, leaning over and kissing her. She kisses him in
           return.)*

DARYL	How do I get past, Rambo?
	(*Dramatic pause. SHONA thinks it through. At last, she takes the swipe card from her neck and gives it to him. He takes it and smiles.*)
DARYL	We'll laugh about this in Italy. You'll see! Have your bags packed. (*DARYL leaves. Off-stage we hear whooping and hollering.*)
DARYL	(*Offstage*) I'M FAT AND I'M FREE!! UP YOURS RAMBO! SEE YOU KEV!!
	(*We hear a screech of tyres then frantic footsteps. GARY and KEVIN tear into the room, breathless.*)
KEVIN	Daryl just gave me the finger from the window of a taxi. What the hell happened?? Why didn't you hit the alarm???
GARY	How did he get past my security measures?
SHONA	I let him go.
GARY	What do you mean 'let him go'?
KEVIN	(*open-mouthed*) You of all people.
GARY	(*spotting the knife*) Was it the knife?
SHONA	Nope. I just let him go.
	(*They sit around stunned, thinking.*)
KEVIN	(*jumping to his feet*) You've betrayed us. That's what you've done!
GARY	How did he do it? What did he say to you? I don't believe this. You were the (*makes quotation marks*) 'brick wall'!
	(*GARY looks around and sees the candles and two plates.*)
GARY	Ahh! I get it. The old honey trap! I bet he told you he

fancied you. That's it, isn't it?

(SHONA looks away.)

GARY   See? What did I tell you, Kev. Weak as piss when it comes right down to it. Bloody women.

KEVIN   I agree with you Gary but calling her 'weak as piss' is not very nice.

GARY   Not nice? Not NICE?? I'll tell you what's not nice! Working us around the clock for three months and not getting paid!

KEVIN   We've already been paid. Remember?

GARY   But we'll have to give it all back when the fat prick's wife sues us for breach.

KEVIN   *(sotto voce)* You of all people...

SHONA   No one's suing anyone. He's not going to tell her. He's going to stay away for a week. She's left him. It's all true.

(GARY collapses laughing.)

GARY   And you fell for that! I suppose he told you that you have perky tits, too.

SHONA   I do have perky tits, Gary. And yes, I actually believe him.

GARY   And I suppose he's going to come back here and sweep you off your feet and you'll both ride off into the sunset.

(SHONA looks away.)

KEVIN   You of all people...

GARY   That's it! That's it!! He's told her he will be back for her, Kev. Well, Shona, I admired you. I even thought you could have cut it in the Special Forces now they've allowed women on the front line.

SHONA	What? And do your tax?
GARY	*(frantic)* He bloody told you!!! He bloody told you! I knew he would.
KEVIN	*(quietly)* No...he didn't, actually. We've known for ages, Gary. It doesn't really matter, anyway.
GARY	Well, it bloody matters to me! I want a discharge.
SHONA	This is not the army, Gary. In real life you say "I quit".
GARY	Okay. I quit. And I'm taking the bloody caravan, too!
SHONA	*(shrugs)* Take it. It's yours.
	(GARY marches from the stage. KEVIN sits in stunned silence.)
KEVIN	*(softly)* Why did you do it, Shona?
	(SHONA hangs her head.)
KEVIN	You know he's lying. You always said they will 'do anything to leave'. They will 'say anything to leave'. You of all people...
SHONA	Will you stop saying *(mock voice)* 'you of all people'. I haven't released a member of a terrorist cell. He's a chubby soft drink salesman.
KEVIN	But why did you do it?
SHONA	*(emotional, teary)* Why? WHY ?? You want to know why? I'll tell you why. Because I want to believe in someone, Kev. I don't actually want to see everybody in my life as a scheming lying bastard. I don't have religion or Zen Buddhism like you do. I have nothing. Nothing but a big black hole. And people emerge and disappear from that big black hole. For once in my life I want to believe in

somebody. Trust somebody. Love somebody. There I've said it. I need to love somebody. Does that make me weak? Does that make me naive?

(KEVIN motions to leave. Pauses at the door.)

KEVIN   You know, I think I understand. I felt like that in the Biggest Loser Couples when Kimberly betrayed me over that vanilla slice. I've never looked at pastry the same way since.

(SHONA chuckles, teary.)

KEVIN   I understand. But I can't do this anymore, either. Not after this. You'll have to find a new partner. It will be hard. I covered a lot of areas: mediation, motivation, diet...

SHONA   *(chuckles)* I won't be replacing you. I'm winding up the business, Kevin.

KEVIN   WHAT?? What will you do?

SHONA   Oh, I've got a little money tucked away. Always wanted to open a secondhand bookshop. Maybe I'll look for a way through that black hole in the pages of those books.

KEVIN   So you knew he was never coming back?

SHONA   Yes. I knew.

BLACKOUT.

END OF SCENE 1

ACT 3
SCENE 2 MOVING ON

Lights are raised. The flat is empty. The wall calendar reveals it is a week later. We hear melancholy music. With drooping shoulders, SHONA is packing up the flat in a series of tall cardboard boxes. We hear a knock at the door.

SHONA   Won't be a minute, Kevin! Keep the car running. This is the last box.

(She opens the door to find DARYL, breathless, dressed in a 'tuxedo T shirt', shorts, and sandals. He is holding a posy of wilting daisies in one hand and two tickets in the other. SHONA is taken aback, jaw drops.)

SHONA   Tickets to Italy?

DARYL   *(panting)* Bernice cleaned me out. Ever stayed in a caravan in Margate?

BLACKOUT

THE END

FURNITURE AND SET PROPERTY LIST
(see SET PLAN)

ACT 1 SCENE 1:	A chair, a table, exercise bike, intercom on wall, panic button (and throughout) on wall, TV/DVD player, CD player, full length mirror, height chart on wall, large wall calendar, video camera on tripod, small row of kitchen units with sink, steel box with mobile in under sink, pedal bin, sign hanging on the wall with blank side outwards (when flipped over it reads DO YOU KNOW HOW MANY LAWS YOU'RE BREAKING?)
ACT 1 SCENE 2:	On table – assorted bowls with foodstuffs, 2 woks, assorted utensils, two ring hob (does not have to be working), can of oil spray, sign saying POUR OIL INTO THE WOK/PAN, the steel box containing the phone is now on the table, teatowel, cloth for wiping down surface.
ACT 2 SCENE 1:	All foodstuffs, hob, utensils etc. removed from table. Exercise Bike moved to front of stage.
ACT 2 SCENE 2:	Exercise Bike moved to one side again. 2 large floor cushions. CD player on floor by cushions.
ACT 2 SCENE 3:	Floor cushions removed. CD player back in original place. Table is laden with food as per script. All food is cleared during the blackout on Page 64. All that is left is the odd half doughnut and broken pie.
ACT 3 SCENE 1:	Table has veg and mushrooms in bowls, hob, kitchen utensils, 2 candles in holders, matches, 2 plates. CD player is moved to where needed by PARIS.
ACT 3 SCENE 2:	Bare, except for kitchen units, wall calendar, cardboard boxes.

PERSONAL PROPERTY LIST

Throughout:	SHONA/GARY/KEVIN have passes on chains around their necks (must be easily detachable though).
ACT 1 SCENE 1:	DARYL – Hood.
	GARY/KEVIN/SHONA – large sports bag, containing : Tuning pipe; party hat; party streamer; bottle of champagne; 3 glasses; contract; sheet of paper (Fattie Fib List); set of scales; large cardboard sign which says THE SCALES ARE WRONG; bag of sugar; BMI booklet; DVD of Bernice; DVD of past clients; photos of past client.
SHONA:	Whistle.
GARY:	Pack of cigarettes.
ACT 1 SCENE 2:	
KEVIN:	Apron, chef's hat.
DARYL:	Apron, chef's hat.
SHONA:	Bag of groceries, handbag, book.
ACT 2 SCENE 1	
GARY:	Paper, pen, combat/SAS equipment (body armour, gloves, gun, balaclava, knife etc.) .
DOUG:	Large iced doughnut, tag around his neck which says WHITECHAPEL ELECTRONICS.
SHONA:	Handbag containing mobile phone.

ACT 2 SCENE 2

DARYL: Flowerpot, garland of flowers around head, mobile
                          phone in pocket.

SHONA/

GARY/KEVIN: Torches.

SHONA: Whistle.

GARY: Club or baseball bat, Chinese takeaway.

ACT 2 SCENE 3

DARYL: Hood.

KEVIN: Bottle of beer, bottle opener.

ACT 3 SCENE 1

SHONA: Book, mobile phone.

ACT 3 SCENE 2

DARYL: Sad bunch of flowers, two tickets.

LIGHTING AND SOUND EFFECTS

ACT 1 SCENE 1:	*Darkness, Arab music. After an agreed period full lights on suddenly – interior, day.*
PAGE 1:	Cue: SHONA: And turn that creepy music off!
	GARY switches off CD player.
PAGE 6:	Cue: SHONA: And...cut!
	Gary feeds DVD into machine.
PAGE 7:	Cue: BERNICE: Love ya, babe!
	GARY switches off DVD
PAGE 11:	Cue: DARYL: The scales are wrong!
	KEVIN hits panic button, siren and red flashing light.
PAGE 12:	Cue: KEVIN: can we play him the testimonials now?
	KEVIN plays DVD.
PAGE 13:	Cue: DARYL: Do you know how many laws you're breaking here?
	KEVIN hits the panic button, siren and red light flashing.
PAGE 18:	Cue: DARYL:...and some Naan bread!
	Blackout.
	Cue: DARYL: Pricks!
	Food related jingles play (or the Fast Food Song?)

ACT 1 SCENE 2	
PAGE 19:	*Fade music, bring up full lights.*
PAGE 21:	Cue: DARYL: Fill the wok with oil.
	Kevin hits the panic button, siren and red flashing light.

PAGE 29:	Cue: DARYL swipes card and exits.
	Siren, red flashing light, electrocution noise, main lights flicker.
	Cue: DARYL: Shit.
	Phone rings inside steel box.
PAGE 31:	Cue: KEVIN: ...silly thing to do nonetheless.
	Intercom buzzes.
PAGE 32:	Cue: KEVIN: Ciao.
	Siren, red flashing light, electrocution noise, main lights flicker.
PAGE 35:	Cue: DARYL: Cracker?
	Blackout. Music plays. (Olivia Newton John "Physical".) Music continues until page 36 unless this is an interval.

ACT 2 SCENE 1

PAGE 36:	*Music fades, bring up full lights.*
PAGE 38:	Cue: DARYL: So is my will to live.
	Intercom buzzes.
PAGE 41:	Cue: DARYL: What did I say?
	Sounds of gunshots offstage.
	Cue: DOUG: ...doing the battalion's taxes. *(laughter)*
	Intercom buzzes.
PAGE 42:	Cue: DOUG: He'll never speak to me again.
	Intercom buzzes again.
PAGE 43:	Cue: GARY: What?
	Intercom buzzes.

PAGE 48:   Cue: DARYL: I know! The last number dialled! *Sound of phone dialling.*

Phone conversation with CHAN which continues until end of page. (Suggest this is done live with CHAN on a mike backstage.)

PAGE 54:   Cue: DARYL: You've got to learn to trust people, Gary.

Blackout. (Possible 'stealth' music. Like 'Pink Panther'?)

ACT 2 SCENE 2

PAGE 55:   *Darkness continues, as per script. Music continues until stage is ready.*

Cue: GARY: Gotcha Piggy!

Eastern meditation music starts. (NOTE: DARYL needs time to get dressed and in position before the lights come up!)

Lights up. Eastern music continues until page 57.

PAGE 57:   Cue: KEVIN: This is hopeless!

KEVIN turns off CD player.

Cue: KEVIN: ...take it seriously, Daryl.

Intercom buzzes. CHAN's voice offstage (on mike) continues as per script.

PAGE 58:   Cue: GARY: Must be Shona.

Mobile in DARYL's pocket rings.

PAGE 62:   Cue: DARYL: Now, where's the chili sauce?

Blackout. Music. (Eric Idle "I like Chinese") Music continues to page 63 unless this is an interval.

ACT 2 SCENE 3

PAGE 63:   *Lights are raised. Music fades.*

PAGE 64:   Cue: SHONA brings her fingers to her eyes then at
                      DARYL as if to say "I'm watching you".

                      *Blackout. Music. ('Food Glorious Food' – could
                      possibly have 'animal-ravaging-food' type noises as
                      well.) Lights are raised and music fades once stage
                      is ready.*

PAGE 67:   Cue: KEVIN chases DARYL around the stage, as
                      he tries to drink it, as DARYL shouts "Willpower!
                      Willpower!"

                      *Blackout. Hip hop dance music could start here
                      and continue to page 68 unless this is an interval.*

ACT 3 SCENE 1

PAGE 68:   *Hip hop music. Lights are raised.*

PAGE 70:   Cue: PARIS: ...and take his hand in yours.

                      Tango music. Play until dance is finished

PAGE 80:   Cue: DARYL: *(Offstage)* SEE YOU KEV!

                      Screech of tyres.

PAGE 83:   Cue: SHONA: Yes I knew.

                      *Blackout. Sad music which continues to page 84.
                      ("I'm Sorry" by Brenda Lee?)*

ACT 3 SCENE 2

PAGE 84:   *Music fades once set is ready. Lights are raised.*

                      Cue: DARYL: ...caravan in Margate?

                      Blackout. Music. ("Physical" again?)

                      Lights raised for curtain calls.

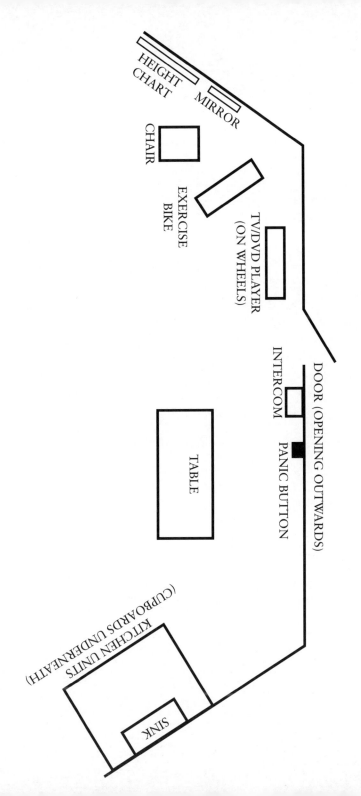

FEEDEM FIGHTERS – SUGGESTED SET PLAN

HEIGHT CHART

MIRROR

CHAIR

EXERCISE BIKE

TV/DVD PLAYER (ON WHEELS)

INTERCOM

DOOR (OPENING OUTWARDS)

PANIC BUTTON

TABLE

KITCHEN UNITS (CUPBOARDS UNDERNEATH)

SINK